HEINKEL
He111
A DOCUMENTARY HISTORY
HEINZ NOWARRA

JANE'S

LONDON · NEW YORK · SYDNEY

First published in 1979 by Motorbuch-Verlag, Stuttgart, as
*Die He 111: Vom Verkehrsflugzeug zum Bomber
1935–1945* © Motorbuch-Verlag, Stuttgart. This English
translation copyright © 1980 Jane's Publishing Company
Limited.

First published in the United Kingdom in 1980 by
Jane's Publishing Company Limited
238 City Road, London EC1V 2PU

ISBN 0 7106 0046 1

Published in the United States of America in 1980 by
Jane's Publishing Inc
730 Fifth Avenue
New York N.Y. 10019

ISBN 0 531 03710 X

Printed in the United Kingdom by
Netherwood Dalton & Co. Ltd.
Huddersfield

HEINKEL
He111
A DOCUMENTARY HISTORY

Contents

Foreword

My special interest in the Heinkel He 111 goes back to February 1939 when I paid another visit to Berlin-Tempelhof airfield. Employed as a junior stock-keeping clerk at Siemens-Schuckert works in Berlin, I was already what is now known as an 'aviation fan' of some standing. I had started spotting aircraft on the many airfields in and around Berlin at the age of fifteen, photographing what appeared to be of interest. I knew of course that it did not do, however, to be caught doing this where Luftwaffe aircraft were concerned—that could turn unpleasant. But it could be done, and I always came prepared.

Someone entering the old Tempelhof airfield had the choice of going to the spectators' area to the left of the terminal, or to that to the right of it. Or one could go up onto the terrace. I had in the past observed that machines with unusual markings, including aircraft used by members of the Luftwaffe or by people today classed as VIPs, were sometimes to be seen in the right-hand area and so I turned right on that occasion. I was not disappointed: two Heinkel 111s were parked there under guard of two SS troopers—in itself a sign of their importance. One of these He 111s was camouflaged and the other bore the registration D-ASAR, but neither had the appearance of Lufthansa machines or of any military aircraft that had been publicly displayed.

To come to the point: it was not until after the war that I was able to identify what I saw there and (as I can now say) secretly photographed as one of the first Heinkel He 111P-series air-craft; D-ASAR served as the official touring aircraft for the then Secretary of State, *Generalleutnant* Erhard Milch. On the occasion of the great parade on the Charlottenburg Chaussee in honour of Hitler's 50th birthday on 20 April 1939, these He 111Ps were among the aircraft in the fly-past. So began my acquaintance with the He 111.

Of course, I had often seen the Lufthansa He 111s at Tempelhof, but these two machines I mentioned were much more interesting. Unfortunately the photographs that I took at Tempelhof were destroyed during an air raid on Berlin on 30 January 1944, but I never lost interest in the aircraft. For years afterwards I have been trying to collect information about the Heinkel 111, and this book is the result of these efforts.

Of course, I could not have succeeded without the help of many other people. Particular thanks, however, are due to the former Ernst Heinkel Werke and their successors VFW-Fokker in Bremen, to my friends Helmuth Roosenboom, Peter Petrick and Rainer Haufschild, to *Major* Bätcher (ret), Gebhard Aders and Mr Jay P. Spenser of the National Air and Space Museum in Washington, USA, and to Deutsche Lufthansa. They have all made photographs and other material available to me in the most selfless fashion and I thank them again most sincerely.

Harreshausen,
23 March 1978

Heinz J. Nowarra

Introduction

The story of the He 111 actually begins in 1922. In that year three students at the College of Technology in Hanover set about constructing an ultra-light glider, the H-6. Their names were Walter Günter, Walter Mertens and Meyer-Cassel. The H-6, which the three of them took to Rhön in 1923 weighed empty only 75 kg (165 lb) and loaded 142 kg (313 lb), a very light design indeed. Here at Rhön the three young students got to know a former First World War fighter pilot, Paul Bäumer, holder of the *Pour-le-Mérite* and with 45 victories to his credit who after the war had founded a firm called 'Bäumer Aero G.m.b.H.' together with another, rather more affluent fighter pilot, Harry von Bülow (after 1939 Commander of II/JG 77 and subsequently *Kommodore* of JG 2 'Richthofen'). Impressed by the H-6 in 1924 Bäumer brought the three men to Hamburg to modify their construction into a powered glider which became known as the Bäumer B I *Roter Vogel* (Red Bird). After this the trio designed an aircraft that can be considered the true ancestor of the He 111, the B II *Sausewind* (Rushing Wind). Looking at this aircraft the ancestry leading from the B II via the B IV to the Heinkel He 64, He 70 and eventually to the He 111 is immediately recognizable.

In 1925 Paul Bäumer flew the B II in the Round-Germany circuit race, achieving second place overall. He covered the competition distance of 5,242 km (3·255 mls) in 91·12 hours, and the aircraft was 29 km/h (18 mph) faster and reached a ceiling 660 m (2,165 ft) higher than its nearest rival. Using a 60 hp engine the B II had a top speed of 170 km/h (105·5 mph),

quite an achievement on so little power. The B II was also remarkable for another reason: it was the first design which involved Walter Günter's twin brother Siegfried. Both Günters continued work on the *Sausewind,* the result being the B IV *Sausewind* which, using an imported American Wright radial engine of only 65 hp, achieved a maximum speed of 230 km/h (143 mph).

On 15 July 1927 Bäumer crashed and was killed over Copenhagen while test-flying the *Rofix,* a single-seat fighter from the Rohrbach-Werke and his firm gradually disintegrated. But the B IV *Sausewind* had been seen and noted by a man who had a particularly 'sensitive nose' for good collaborators: Ernst Heinkel.

Heinkel invited first Siegfried and then Walter Günter to join him in Warnemünde. In his memoirs he gave a good description of the twin brothers: 'For my purposes they complemented each other in an almost ideal fashion. Siegfried was the 'mathematical technician', Walter more the artist with an uncanny feel for the aesthetic beauty of an aircraft and this meant it being shaped for speed . . . Both Siegfried and Walter were theoreticians who did not fly themselves and appeared to be incapable of practical work. But they had a 'certain something' . . . These two brothers could co-ordinate the details of the rough plans I had in my mind. They combined a gift for mathematical precision with a feeling for aesthetic beauty: they were capable of creating the aerodynamic shape I was looking for.' Heinkel was really not so much a true designer of aircraft as a man of ideas. He knew how to find and employ the right men to carry out his ideas and was a good organizer and, above all, an outstanding businessman. Already at that time he made use of 'market research' in its most modern sense. He learnt from a report by the German Aviation Experimental Establishment (*Deutsches Versuchsanstalt für Luftfahrt* or DVL), that mail aircraft were being built in America capable of substantially increased speeds due not only to more powerful engines but also to outstandingly good aerodynamic design and to retractable undercarriages, and

he sent Siegfried Günter to the USA to find out what was actually happening.

Siegfried Günter came back and reported to his chief on what he had seen, ending his account with the words: 'But we shall need to be very quick about it, *Herr* Heinkel'. Thus began Heinkel's first attempt to draw level with the Americans.

Bäumer B.II/IV, the Günther brothers' first design

Left to right: Ernst Heinkel, Siegfried and Walter Günter

Heinkel He 64 'Roter Teufel' (Red Devil)

From 1930 onwards there was an annual International Round-Europe Race, the *Europa Rundflug.* In 1930 and 1931 the winners were the Messerschmitt designs M 23b and M 32c flown by Fritz Morzik (later Chief of Luftwaffe transport aviation during the Second World War). Heinkel decided to compete with a new aircraft for the 1932 Round-Europe Race, a design that for the first time would embody the

Günters' ideas, but no attempt was made as yet to tackle a retractable undercarriage; that still had to be developed and tested.

It was clear to all concerned that improved performance was the main requirement for the 1932 Round-Europe Race. Until 1931 the 7,600 km (4,658 mile) circuit had been covered in 12 days; it was now considered feasible to cover the distance in only 6 days. The Günter brothers' new design was given the designation He 64. Everyone who saw the new aircraft was impressed by its unusually slim and elegant shape. The fuselage had an oval cross-section and the cockpit was completely enclosed by an aerodynamically designed *Cellon* cover. The He 64 was powered by an Argus As 8R inline engine with a take-off power of 150 hp and had a nominal rating of 135 hp, and the three aircraft entered in the Round-Europe Race were all painted red. Although not the winner, which had something to do with the peculiar competition rules, the He 64 was the technical sensation of this Round-Europe Race.

In the hot August days of 1932 the present writer, like so many other Germans, was glued to the radio and closely followed the latest news of the race's progress. Now came the first mention of the name of this aircraft, the Red Devil, and the name of the man linked with it: Hans Seidemann. He was to show his competitive spirit again at Zürich in 1937. Later, Seidemann gave proof of his abilities as Chief of Staff to the last commander of the *Legion Condor* in Spain in 1938/39 and on many fronts during the Second World War, rising to the rank of *Generalmajor* as the last *Fliegerführer Afrika.*

Seidemann was greeted with a storm of enthusiasm when, on 27 August 1932 he landed his 'Red Devil' at Berlin-Staaken. He had not taken six days to cover the 7,500 km circuit as expected, but had streaked like a demon round Europe. In the very first stage from Berlin via Warsaw, Prague and Vienna to Rome he outstripped all the other competitors. The Italians had expected their entrant to reach Rome first and were naturally bitterly disappointed. At first the Italian, Colombo (in a Breda), and Seidemann were neck and neck but then the German pilot drew ahead and left his rival behind. The next morning he started on the second stage via Florence, Nice, Lyons, Stuttgart and Bonn to Paris. In Paris no one expected any of the Round-Europe pilots to arrive so early and the aerodrome staff had gone home. Suddenly the hum of an engine was heard and Seidemann's red aircraft was approaching to land. A couple of reporters were still there, sensing a scoop, and the next morning all the papers carried the headline: 'Red Devil outstrips everyone!' But Seidemann wanted to be certain. The next morning he shot off again and flew via Amsterdam, Copenhagen, Göteburg and Hamburg back to Berlin. Thus he had covered the course, timed for six days, in only three and had pushed up the speed record for the Round-Europe Race to 240 km/hr (149 mph)—and that with an engine nominally rated at 135 hp! However, the He 64 was not only fast but could, if required, fly slowly: it could remain in the air at a speed of 62·3 km/hr (39 mph) without stalling and had a landing speed of 52 km/hr (32 mph). It seems unlikely that any similarly powered modern sports aircraft is capable of such performance.

The He 64a, the first prototype, crashed during trials. The version competing in the Round-Europe Race was designated He 64B. Its subsequent developments were the He 64C, an export version with the British de Havilland Gypsy III engine, and the He 64D. Only two examples of the He 64D were built, and these had new wings already closely resembling those of the later He 70. With an As 8R engine the He 64D reached a top speed of 295 km/hr (183 mph). This proved that they were working on the right lines and the battle to reduce the American lead was truly joined.

The victorious Heinkel He 64, the
'Red Devil' of the 1932
Round-Europe Race. *Below:* Its
pilot Hans Seidemann (2nd from
right) with the Heinkel team

13

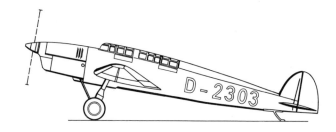

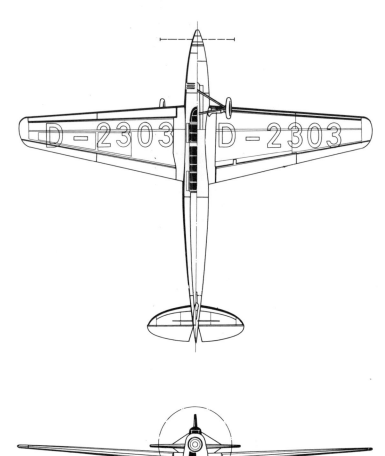

Heinkel He 70 Blitz (Lightning)

In 1931 Lockheed brought out a new, single-engined mail aircraft with a 500 hp engine said to be capable of reaching a speed of 260 km/hr (162 mph) at an all-up flying weight of 2,360 kg (5,203 lb). In Germany, at this time, the highest speed that had been obtained was 220 km/hr (137 mph). Heinkel followed the technical press and read the reports on the new Lockheed Orion with great interest and he also saw the potential of this machine equipped with a retractable under-carriage. At Lufthansa the man responsible for all technical matters at the time was Dipl. Ing. Schatzki. Schatzki was a Jew and after the Nazi takeover in 1933 was purged in an unpleasant fashion, as was Director Wronski who was also not a 'pure aryan'.

Schatzki had seen the He 64 and had also heard about Lockheed Orion. Meeting Heinkel by chance in Unter-den-Linden he spoke to him about the American aircraft. Heinkel merely told him that Lufthansa should look out for something better, but his mind was working. He already planned to develop the He 64 further, but he had to think of the business side of it: what he needed was someone to buy the aircraft and cover the costs. Erhard Milch, the Director of Lufthansa, had close connections with the Junkers factory, and had already placed an order with Junkers for an aircraft to compete with the Orion. Junkers, however,

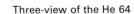

Three-view of the He 64

Lockheed 9D Orion

Junkers Ju 60

Left: Schatzki, Technical Director of Lufthansa

Right: Erhard Milch, Chief of Lufthansa

15

were going through a financial crisis which was to lead to the expropriation of Professor Hugo Junkers himself and to the business being taken over by the state. Heinkel had never worked for Lufthansa but was, nonetheless, well-known in the *Reichsverkehrsministerium,* the State Ministry of Transport. Heinkel had built military aircraft for the Reichswehr which was strictly illegal under the terms of the 1919 Treaty of Versailles. And the man who placed these, albeit heavily camouflaged contracts, was *Ministerialrat* (Counsellor) Brandenburg, who had commanded *Bombengeschwader* 3 that had raided London during the First World War and who was now Head of the Reich Ministry of Transport Aviation Division. In February 1932 he invited Heinkel to visit him and asked him whether he could build an aircraft approximately equivalent to the Lockheed Orion in about six months. Heinkel immediately answered 'Yes', but was of the opinion that the aircraft must be capable of 320 km/hr at least since, by the time the German machine was ready, the Americans would certainly again have increased their speed. Brandenburg did not think that this would be possible and wanted to talk it over first with his experts and Director Milch.

On 12 February 1932 a decisive discussion took place between Brandenburg, Milch, Schatzki and Heinkel and Lufthansa placed an order for a fast aircraft with a crew of two pilots and carrying four passengers.

The top speed required was 285 km/hr (177 mph). No one was prepared to believe that Heinkel could possibly build an aircraft of this description capable of flying at over 320 km/hr (199 mph).

Heinkel returned to Warnemünde and the Günter brothers started work. On 15 May 1932 there was a press report that Swissair had bought the Lockheed Orion. Heinkel immediately got in touch with the Berlin officials and described the position as it now stood. Milch recognized that Heinkel was right and agreed to a speed of over 300 km/hr (186 mph); Brandenburg also gave the project his blessing. At Warnemünde work now went on at full speed: four weeks saw the completion of the specifications, costings and the general drawings for a 'high-speed civil and mail aircraft', the He 70—with a guaranteed top speed of 314 km/hr (195 mph). Schatzki and Achterberg, his assistant, remained sceptical. They could not believe it possible to build such an aircraft without a lengthy process of development, but Heinkel proved them wrong.

Walter Günter designed a low-winged aircraft of most attractive shape featuring retractable undercarriage and tail-skid. The power plant chosen was the most powerful in-line engine available in Germany at that time, the 12-cylinder BMW VI, glycol- instead of water-cooled, with a take-off rating of 637 hp. Lockheed had used an air-cooled radial engine which, despite of its NACA cowling, offered greater drag than the in-line engine which in addition was fitted with a retractable radiator.

As far as the airframe was concerned, the Günter brothers had completely discarded traditional methods of construction and had chosen one that was to prove a landmark in airframe construction. The State Ministry of Transport approved the design on 14 June 1932. A bare six months later a prototype, the He 70a, was ready and was brought to Travemünde for its test flights since the airfield at the Heinkel Works in Warnemünde appeared to be too small.

Test flights were to be carried out by Werner Junck, at that time the Heinkel Works Chief Test Pilot. (In the Second World War Junck

16

The first He 70 shortly after completion

Flugkapitän Untucht (left) in front of the He 70 after the demonstration at Berlin-Tempelhof

17

became an *Oberst* and was prominent as a fighter leader with *Luftflotte* 3 during the Battle of Britain). The Heinkel Works celebrated their 10th anniversary on 1 December 1932 and on the previous day Junck and Heinkel's old colleague 'Jupp' Köhler carried out the first runway tests with the new machine. Köhler was so conscientious that he hung on to the undercarriage to make sure that it was firm enough. It must be remembered that no one as yet had any experience of retractable undercarriages, since the He 70 was the first German aircraft to be fitted with one.

A telephone line had been laid from Travemünde to Warnemünde so that those in Warnemünde could be kept informed as to how the first flight had gone, and the instrument at that end was now besieged by Heinkel, the Günter brothers, Köhler, Schwärzler (the head of the construction office) and many others. Junck started up the He 70a in Warnemünde, took off well and, to everyone's relief, landed in Travemünde fifteen minutes later. Then came the day of the speed trials. Junck returned beaming from this first flight to be exclusively devoted to attaining the highest speed possible. 'At least 360 km/hr! But I think there's more to be got out of it. It's a marvellous bird. . .' It turned out that the aircraft could fly with full load at 377 km/hr (234 mph).

Now the He 70 went to Deutsche Lufthansa (DLH) at Staaken and was officially licensed. *Flugkapitän* (Flight Captain) Untucht of DLH was the man who made the He 70 popular: in the period between 13 March and 28 April 1933 Untucht captured eight international records for Germany with the second prototype aircraft, the D-3 (later D-2357)—records that up till then had been held by the French and the Americans. Heinkel himself wrote: 'The most important were the records with 500 and 1,000

kg payloads over a distance of 1,000 km and here a speed of 357·427 km/hr (222 mph) was reached.' The previous records held by France and the USA were 298 and 299 km/hr (185 mph and 185·8 mph respectively). The significance of these records is emphasised by the fact that in 1933 the absolute world record for land-aircraft was only 417·06 km/hr (259·15 mph). This had, however, been achieved with a purpose-built specialized machine while the He 70 was a normal Lufthansa mail aircraft.

The military, took this very seriously. The fastest French fighter had a speed of a little over 300 km/hr (186 mph). Reginald J. Mitchell, the designer of the Spitfire wrote to Heinkel: 'We, at Supermarine Aviation, were particularly impressed, since we have been unable to achieve such smooth lines in the aircraft that we entered for the Schneider Trophy Races . . . In addition to this, we recently investigated the effect that installing certain new British fighter engines would have on the He 70. We were dismayed to find that your aircraft, despite its larger measurements, is appreciably faster than our fighters. It is indeed a triumph.'

It is only when one compares pictures of the He 70 and the Spitfire in flight that one can appreciate how strong was the influence of the He 70 on the original design of the Spitfire. The Japanese also closely followed this design when developing their new aircraft, particularly the Mitsubishi A5M and the Aichi D3A1.

But the officers who at this time — albeit under cover — were building up the new German Air Force — tended to be more reactionary and conservative in their thinking. At the time all single-seat fighters being built for the Luftwaffe were biplanes and all were appreciably slower than this mail aircraft. It was not until after the He 70 had appeared that *Oberst* Wimmer, the head of the Technical Office of

These pictures of the He 70 and a Spitfire Mk IX in flight clearly show the influence that the He 70 had on the design of the British fighter

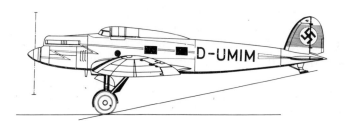

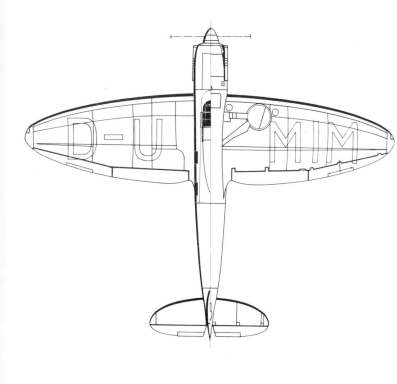

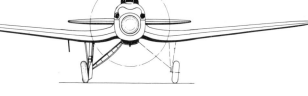

Three-view of the He 70G built for Lufthansa

the then *Luftfahrtkommissariat* (Aviation Commissariat) which later became the *Reichsluftfahrtministerium* or RLM (State Aviation Ministry) issued a requirement for a modern single-seat fighter, which had to be a monoplane, preferably of metal construction, with retractable undercarriage and be capable of reaching 450 km/hr (279·6 mph) with a 650 hp engine. This in due course led to the development of the Arado Ar 80, Focke-Wulf Fw 159, Heinkel He 112 and 100 and, ultimately, to the Messerschmitt Bf 109.

Now that the He 70 was about to go into airline service with Lufthansa some quick thinking had to be done. By order of the new Aviation Commissariat which had been set up under Göring when the National Socialists came to power, the fourth He 70 prototype, He 70 V4 D-UHYS was converted into a fast reconnaissance aircraft. Several aircraft of this type were built for the Luftwaffe but they proved to be unsuitable for service use. In 1934 a new military version appeared, the He 70F-1, about 60 of which were built. In 1937 the *Aufklärungsruppen* 121 (Neuhausen), 123 (Grossenhain), 124 (Kassel), 125 (Würzburg) and 127 (Goslar) each consisted of nine He 70F-1 and 27 He 45 biplanes. The He 70 was used for long-range reconnaissance and the He 45 for tactical tasks. In 1936 several He 70F-1s were sent to Spain and were employed with *Aufklärungsgruppe* A/88 of *Legion Condor.* Their performance there however did not prove entirely satisfactory, since their maintenance under operational conditions proved too difficult. As a result, the He 70Fs were soon replaced in the reconnaissance role by the Dornier Do 17F, at home as well as in Spain. The He 70s sent to Spain were already the F-2 series and were later handed over to the Spanish *Grupo* 7-G-14.

The He 70V4 modified as a reconnaissance aircraft

The new *Reichskommissar* for Aviation Hermann Göring after inspecting the successful He 70. *Left to right:* (3rd) Milch, (4th) von Pfistermeister, Heinkel's representative in Berlin, (5th) Christiansen, and (6th) Göring

21

In spring 1936 one He 70G was equipped with a Rolls Royce Kestrel V engine and delivered to Britain. This aircraft originally bore the registration D-UBOF but was later given the British civil registration G-ADZF. The background to this arrangement was that Heinkel had originally wanted to do an exchange deal with Britain: permission to build the He 70 against the right to build the Rolls Royce engines under licence. This deal was turned down by the German government, allegedly for political reasons. It is more likely, however, that this was done for prestige reasons. Daimler-Benz were already working on the DB 600 and Junkers on the Jumo 210; what point was there for anyone to build British engines under licence?

In the meantime, the He 70 was developed into the He 170 powered by the French 910 hp Gnome-Rhône 14K Mistral-Major twin-row radial engine. Twenty machines of this version were exported to Hungary in 1937-38 (where their engines were licence-built by Manfred Weiss at Budapest) and flown on active service by the Hungarian Air Force until 1941. The final development was the He 270 powered by a 1,175 hp Daimler-Benz DB 601Aa engine. Although appreciably faster than its predecessors, the He 270 was never built in series because the Luftwaffe now insisted on twin-engined bombers and reconnaissance aircraft.

In all, 296 He 70, He 170 and He 270 were built, which amply justified Heinkel's original investment in the He 70 development.

The He 70 had barely gone into airline service with Lufthansa before the Günter brothers were working on another aircraft which was destined to make aviation history. The new design was to be just one size larger.

Meanwhile however something had happened, the consequences of which were not to be apparent until later. On 3 June 1936 the Chief of the General Staff of the Luftwaffe, *Generalleutnant* Wever crashed and was killed at Dresden-Neustadt in an He 70 belonging to the RLM. Wever at this time was certainly the most competent General Staff officer in the Luftwaffe, but had not learnt to fly himself until 1934/35. He had chosen the fast He 70 as his official communications aircraft, but, being a comparative flying novice, he was unable to completely master such an ultra-modern type as the He 70 then was.

In the cockpit of the He 70 there was a lever for securing the ailerons while the machine was parked. Every pilot, before taking off, operates all controls to check their functions. Somehow Wever forgot this lever, resulting in an accident that seemed inexplicable and the cause of which was not discovered until later. With the death of this man the development of the Luftwaffe took a different course from that originally planned. There was also a curious thing about Wever's death that went unnoticed at the time: the official and press announcements of his death all refered to him as *'Generalstabschef der Luftwaffe'*. Officially, there was at that time no such appointment. Even after his death, on 1 July 1936, the official description of his appointment in the Establishment Lists of the RLM read *'Chef des Luftkommandoamtes* (LA). The appointment of 'Chief of the General Staff of the Luftwaffe' does not appear in the RLM organisation until 1 July 1937, which in no way alters the fact that Wever actually was Chief of the General Staff at the time of his death.

Above: He 70F-1 of 3.(F)/123 long-range reconnaissance *Staffel*
Below: An He 70F-2 in service with the *Legion Condor* ▶

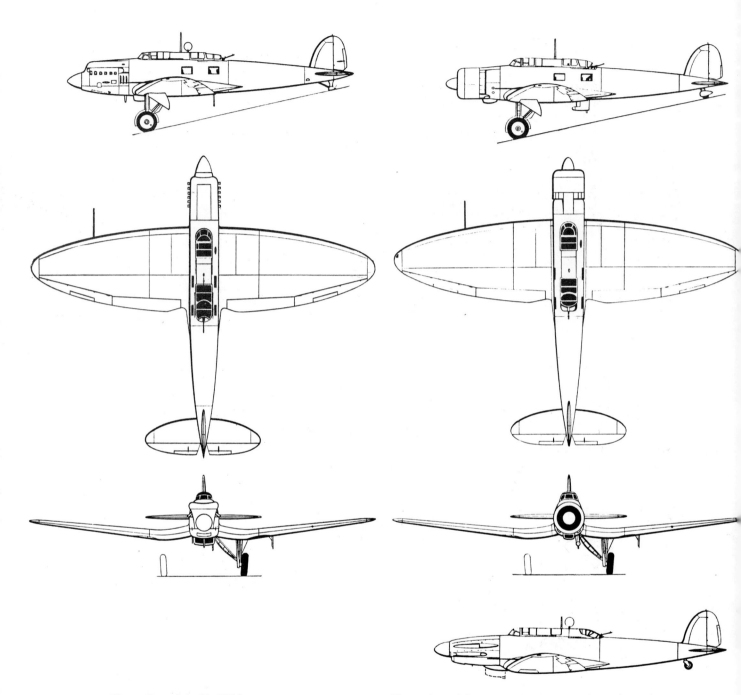

Three-view of the He 70F-2

Three-view of the He 170 (top), with a side-view of the He 270

24

Above: A Gnome-Rhône 14K-powered He 170, one of 18 delivered to Hungary in 1937/38.
Below: The sole DB 601Aa-powered He 270

Heinkel He 70s in DLH (Deutsche Lufthansa) service

Identification letters	Work No.	Type	Name	Identification letters	Work No.	Type	Name
D-2537	403	He 70a	originally D-3 *Blitz* (Lightning)	D-UJUZ	909	He 70G-1	*Bussard* (Buzzard)
				D-UKEK	928	He 70G-1	*Amsel* (Blackbird)
D-3114	457	He 70A	Later D-UBAF *Sperber* (Sparrow Hawk)	D-UMIM	917	He 70G-1	*Albatros* (Albatross)
				D-UNEH	912	He 70G-1	*Kondor* (Condor)
				D-UPYF	910	He 70G-1	*Adler* (Eagle)
D-UBIN	709	He 70D-0	*Falke* (Falcon)	D-UQIP	913	He 70G-1	*Rabe* (Raven)
D-UBOX	911	He 70G-1	*Geier* (Vulture)	D-USAZ	914	He 70G-1	*Buntspecht* (Woodpecker)
D-UDAS	710	He 70D-0	*Habicht* (Goshawk)				
D-UGOR	711	He 70D-0	*Schwalbe* (Swallow)	D-UXUV	916	He 70G-1	*Drossel* (Thrush)

Heinkel He 111: the benign beginning

In June 1933 a certain *Herr* Albert Kesselring turned up at the Heinkel factory — in civilian clothes, naturally enough. There was as yet no State Aviation Ministry but an Aviation Commissariat, the *Luftfahrtkommissariat*. In this organisation Kesselring was head of the Luftwaffe Administration Office (LD) with the Reichswehr rank of *Oberst*. He was one of those officers who hoped to create an air force out of the nucleus flying corps that had been built up clandestinely within the Reichswehr. One of the most important tasks to be undertaken was that of creating new capacities for the mass-production of aircraft and new engines, and this was mainly Kesselring's responsibility. At that time he was 48, an energetic 'live wire' but with a pleasant personality. His aim was to persuade Heinkel to give up the factory at Warnemünde and to establish a new one near Rostock, capable initially of employing a workforce of 3,000. But neither Kesselring nor Heinkel were at that time to know that this number was to prove too limited and that continual enlargements of the factory which grew up on the Marienehe estate on the banks of the Warnow would mean that it would never quite be finished.

Rostock-Marienehe was the birthplace of the He 111, the first aircraft to be produced in the new factory. In addition to this, it was the first aircraft employing all-metal construction to be built by Heinkel.

Lufthansa wanted to increase its fleet of fast aircraft, and the new machine they wanted was to carry ten passengers and had to be multi-engined. In principle, Lufthansa already were quite satisfied with the three-engined Junkers machine, the Ju 52/3m, but at Heinkel's people had already seen details of the new American models which were all twin-engined: the Lockheed 12, Boeing 247, and Douglas DC-2. Lufthansa's development order was placed in 1934, a similar order being placed simultaneously with Junkers where a twin-engined aircraft was also to be built. In the background, backing up the Lufthansa commission stood the *Technische Amt des RLM* or Technical Office of the State Aviation Ministry (LC). Both Junkers and Heinkel received instructions to build a machine that could equally well be used as a civil or military aircraft. Whereas, however, the Ju 86V1 had clearly recognisable provisions for armament, in the He 111a these were concealed (the designation V1 was not used until later). Only the glazed nose gave any clue as to the aircraft's military potential. The Günter brothers again produced the initial design which was then taken over by Karl Schwärzler, head of the construction office, who completed the detail design. In contrast to experience with the He 70 there was enough time to subject the He 111 to critical examination in the wind tunnel. Heinkel — and also Junkers — would apparently never have

The crisp clean lines of the Administrative block of the new Heinkel works at Rostock-Marienehe reflected the activities within

Prof Ernst Heinkel and his Chief Designer Karl Schwärzler

27

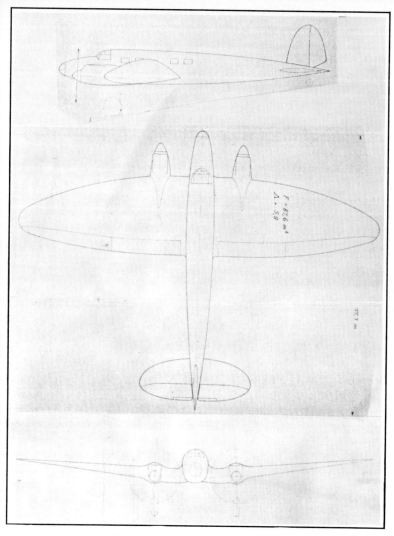

The original draft for the initial He 111 design

accepted the commission unless there had been the prospect of orders for a series production as bombers for the Luftwaffe: a Lufthansa order for at the most a dozen aircraft, would never have covered development costs. The situation at that time was very similar to that in the USA after the Second World War where the development of the Boeing KC-135 jet transport and tanker aircraft covered part of the development costs of the Boeing 707 airliner.

Germany still had no German-built aero engines developing more than 600 hp continuous power and so they had to make do with the glycol-cooled BMW VI for the He 111 as well.

The airfield at Marienehe was only partially completed when, on 24 February 1935 the He 111a was rolled out for its first flight. Werner Junck, the former Chief test pilot had, in the meantime, transferred to the Luftwaffe. His successor was a 30-year-old East Prussian named Gerhard Nitschke.

Nitschke had been a member of the Reichswehr and, as such, had received his training as a fighter pilot in the secret German air-base at Lipetzk in the Soviet Union under Carl-August von Schoenebeck, a former First World War fighter squadron commander. Afterwards he worked at the German civil flying school at List on the island of Sylt.

Before Nitschke took off on the first flight in the He 111, Heinkel himself urged him to land at Rechlin, since the landing strip at Marienehe was still too short. The He 111 seemed to be very fast which would make its landing speed too high for Marienehe. Nitschke agreed and nodded. Then he climbed into the cockpit and taxied to the start. Take-off went according to plan and the aircraft rose elegantly. Then Nitschke began to bank, to dive and to climb steeply — everything worked, and the speed of it was fascinating. All the more reason, reckoned Heinkel, to land in Rechlin. But, to his astonishment and with a certain amount of anxiety he watched while Nitschke did a wide, banking turn and came in to land. He flattened

Above: The He 111a, later designated He 111V1, made its first flight on 24 February 1935. *Below:* The He 111V2 D-ALIX ▶

28

ROSTOCK D-ALIX

out slowly, touched down and then taxied calmly to the hangar. As soon as he had climbed out of the machine he exclaimed with satisfaction: 'I noticed at once in the air when throttling back that the bird had excellent landing characteristics!' These characteristics remained throughout the whole development of the He 111 as all who flew it still testify today.

Four weeks later the He 111V2 D-ALIX completed its first flight and then went to Staaken to be put through an intensive programme of tests. Later it was incorporated into the Lufthansa fleet with the name *Rostock*. The next prototype aircraft, He 111V3 D-ALES then became the prototype of the first bomber version, the He 111A-1.

The He 111V4 D-AHAO in turn became the prototype for the Lufthansa C-0 series and this was the first machine to be publicly unveiled on 10 January 1936 when Nitschke demonstrated it for the German and foreign press at Berlin-Tempelhof. He flew full-throttle, in slow flight, with one engine only, banking and climbing steeply to the wholehearted enthusiasm of all present. Headlines in the press announced: 'The fastest aircraft on the world's air-routes', or 'New achievement by the German aircraft industry', or 'The He 111 breaks the 400 km barrier'. This last was not true, though: the He 111 was only able to achieve this with the new Daimler-Benz DB 600 engines which developed 900 hp. The good old 750 hp BMW VIU could not be made to pull the aircraft along at more than 345 km/hr (214 mph). D-AHAO was given the name *Dresden* and had the *Werk Nr.* 1968. If one takes into account that the He 111V2, the second prototype, still had the works number 715 one can get some idea of the rate at which aircraft were being produced by the Heinkel factory at this time. In 1938 Lufthansa received a new version

of the He 111, the G-0. This differed from the C-0 in having a new wing with a straighter leading edge like the one that had been introduced on the He 111V7 prototype bomber version. Two of these aircraft were fitted with BMW 132Dc radial engines and classed as G-3s. These were the so-called 'quick-change power units' which could also be fitted to the Junkers Ju 90 and consisted of an engine in its cowling which could be changed over complete. Of the He 111 G-4 only the prototype aircraft was not taken over by Lufthansa. This He 111G with DB 600 engines was given the prototype number V16 and became the official communications aircraft of the Secretary of State Erhard Milch.

In all the following aircraft were handed over to *Lufthansa:*

Works Number	Registration	Name	Version
715	D-ALIX	*Rostock*	V2
1828	D-AMES	*Nürnberg*	C-0
1829	D-AQYF	*Leipzig*	C-0
1830	D-AXAF	*Köln*	C-0
1831	D-ABYE	*Königsberg*	C-0
1832	D-AQUA	*Breslau*	C-0
1833	D-ATYL	*Karlsruhe*	C-0
1884	D-ACBS	*Augsburg*	G-3
1885	D-ADCF	*Dresden*	G-3
1968	D-AHAO	*Dresden*	V4
2534	D-AEQA	*Halle*	G-1
2535	D-AYKI	*Magdeburg*	G-1

The He 111C-0 first went into service on the Berlin-Hanover-Amsterdam, the Berlin-Nuremberg-Munich and the Berlin-Dortmund-Cologne routes, later being used on

Three views of the first bomber version, the He 111V3, prototype for the He 111A-series ▶

◀ *Left:* The He 111V4 D-AHAO was the prototype aircraft for the He 111C-series for Lufthansa

▲ *Above:* He 111C-0 *Werk Nr.* 1829 D-AQYF *Leipzig*

▼ *Below:* He 111C-0 *Werk Nr.* 1832 D-AQUA *Breslau*

This aerial shot of the He 111C-0 Werk Nr. 1830 *Köln* shows to particular advantage the outstanding aerodynamic lines of the airframe designed by the Günter brothers. *Right:* This photograph of the well-appointed cabin interior of the He 111C shows that nothing was lacking for passenger comfort

sixteen different routes. The He 111V3 began flying on the European section of the South Atlantic mail route. The section Berlin-Danzig-Königsberg in the network of the German-Soviet Air Transport Company *Deruluft* was also flown with an He 111.

Further, it should be noted that a whole series of Lufthansa aircraft were converted in 1938/39 to the He 111 G-3 version. They were fitted with the standard BMW 132H power units and, in the case of the C-aircraft, the G-series type wings. Apparently only a few non-military aircraft were built after the G-4 version and these were used by the official Reich authorities, for example D-ADNH (*Werk Nr.* 2471) and D-ADBX which served the Reich Foreign Ministry.

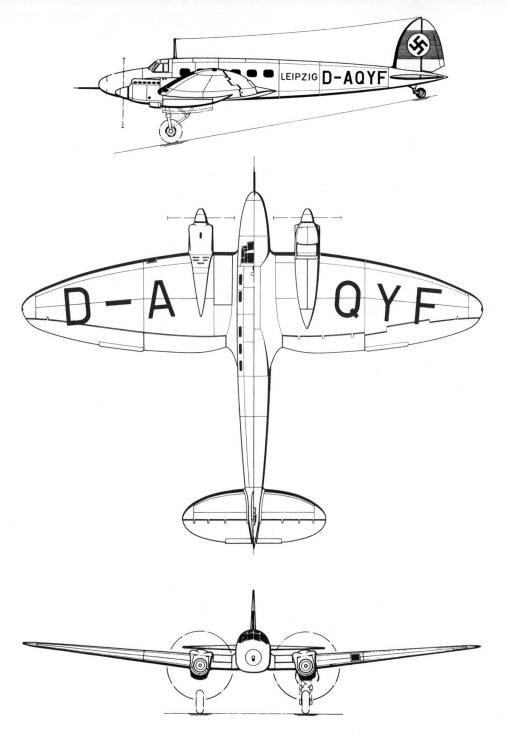

Three-view of the He 111C-0

35

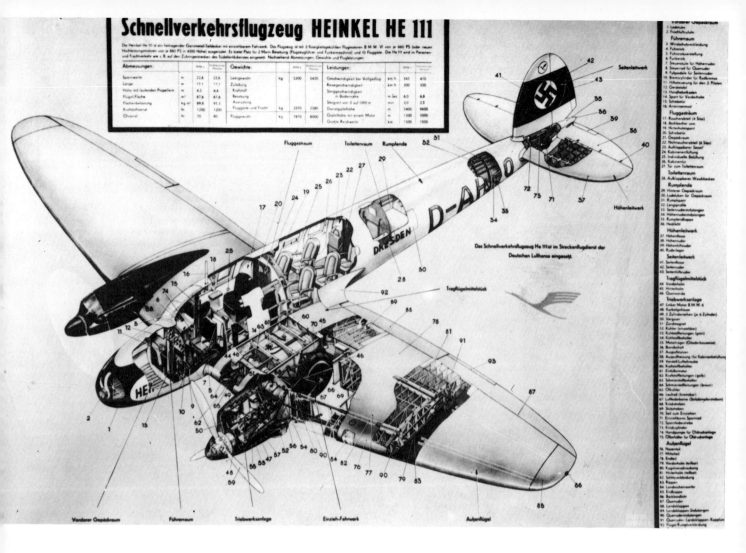

The diagram bears the heading **Schnellverkehrsflugzeug HEINKEL HE 111**, with the aircraft registration **D-AHAO** and *DRESDEN* / *HEIN* markings visible. The German label list on the right and various numbered callouts are part of the drawing.

Above: A contemporary cutaway drawing of the He 111V4
D-AHAO *Dresden*

◀ The only two representatives of the He 111G-1 series,
D-AEQA and D-AYKI. The side view shows the new wing
shape used from the F-1 series onwards particularly well.

Above and left: Two He 111G-3s with the BMW 132 H 'quick change' engines

Right: He 111 D-ASAR served for a long time as the personal communications aircraft for Erhard Milch

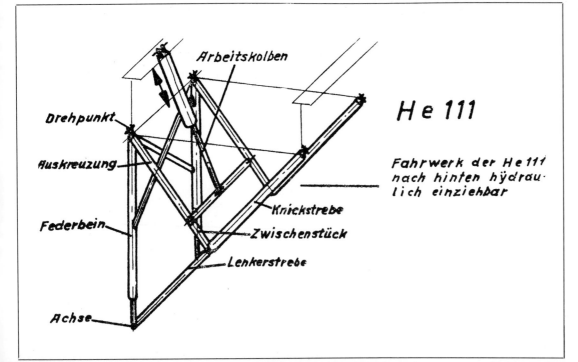

He 111

Fahrwerk der He 111
nach hinten hydrau-
lich einziehbar

Arbeitskolben

Drehpunkt

Auskreuzung

Federbein

Knickstrebe

Zwischenstück

Lenkerstrebe

Achse

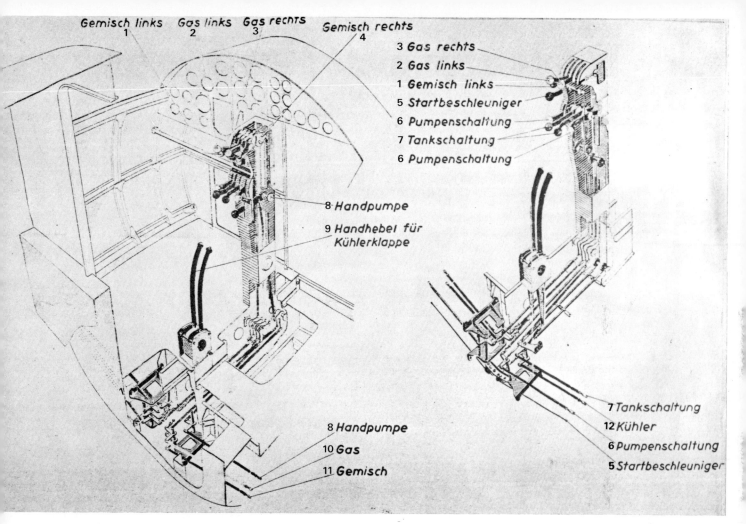

Gemisch links 1 Gas links 2 Gas rechts 3 Gemisch rechts 4

3 Gas rechts
2 Gas links
1 Gemisch links
5 Startbeschleuniger
6 Pumpenschaltung
7 Tankschaltung
6 Pumpenschaltung

8 Handpumpe
9 Handhebel für Kühlerklappe

8 Handpumpe
10 Gas
11 Gemisch

7 Tankschaltung
12 Kühler
6 Pumpenschaltung
5 Startbeschleuniger

Key

Diagram of the engine operating controls

1. Left mixture
2. Left throttle
3. Right throttle
4. Right mixture
5. Take-off accelerator
6. Fuel pump switch (regulator)
7. Fuel tank switch
8. Manual pump
9. Hand lever for operating radiator flaps
10. Throttle
11. Fuel mixture
12. Radiator

Main undercarriage unit

1. Knee joint
2. Support strut
3. Hinged bearings
4. Axle knee joints
5. Wheel axle
6. Telescopic leg
7. Cross-bracing for the telescopic leg

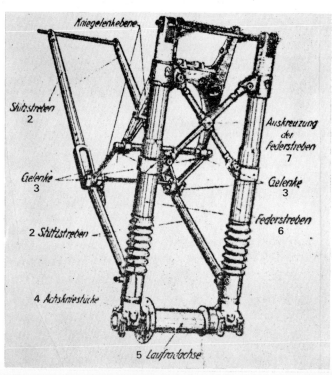

Kniegelenkebene

Stützstreben
2

Auskreuzung
der
Federstreben
7

Gelenke
3

Gelenke
3

2 Stützstreben

Federstreben
6

4 Achskniestücke

5 Laufradachse

He 111G-5 destined for Turkey
Left: He 111V16 in military guise as courier aircraft

Side views of the He 111C-0, He 111G-3, He 111B-2 and He 111E-3 ▶

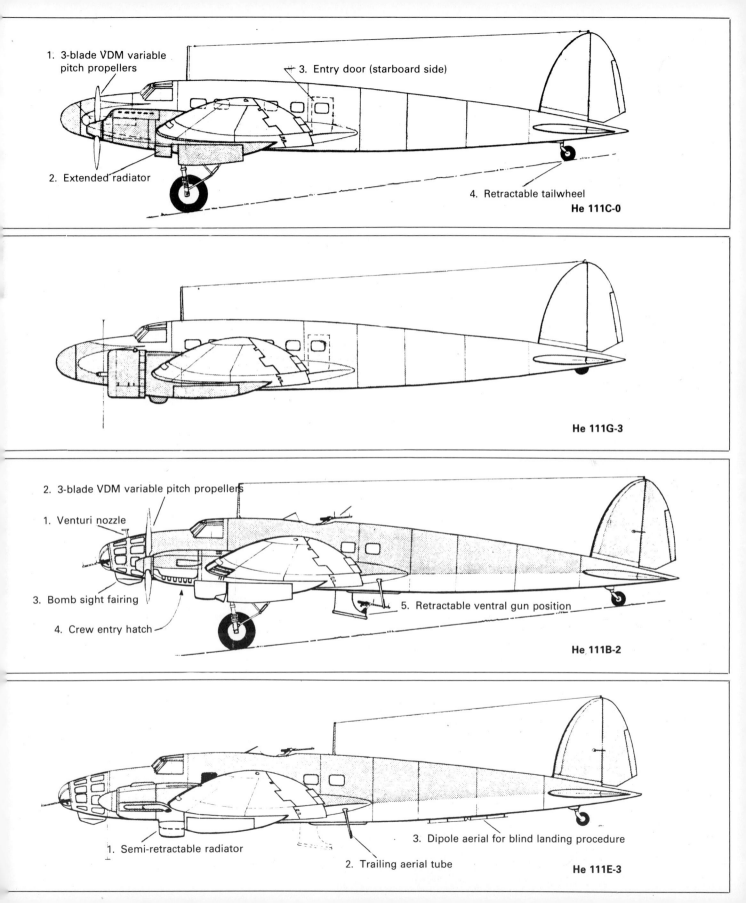

1. 3-blade VDM variable pitch propellers

3. Entry door (starboard side)

2. Extended radiator

4. Retractable tailwheel

He 111C-0

He 111G-3

2. 3-blade VDM variable pitch propellers

1. Venturi nozzle

3. Bomb sight fairing

4. Crew entry hatch

5. Retractable ventral gun position

He 111B-2

1. Semi-retractable radiator

2. Trailing aerial tube

3. Dipole aerial for blind landing procedure

He 111E-3

Into Luftwaffe service

Once the performance of the He 111 had been publicly demonstrated in the display at Tempelhof it was up to the Luftwaffe to make the next move. Performance with the BMW VI engines was acceptable, but something even better was required. The test flights of the He 111 V3 at Rechlin had gone satisfactorily, but plans had been made for a bomber actually capable of flying at over 400 km/hr and no interest was shown in the He 111A-0 series for which the V3 was the prototype. Ernst Heinkel, however, was a businessman and, to some extent, had a pretty elastic conscience. He had always worked well with the Japanese who were building the He 50 dive bomber as Aichi D1A2, and later a modified He 65/He 70 as the Aichi D3A1. Heinkel had also built the first carrier-based aircraft for the Japanese Navy, the HD 25 and 26 and some fleet spotters such as the HD 28. Now however Japan's opponents — the Chinese government of Chiang-kai-shek, came to him wanting to buy aircraft, and, what is more, they wanted the He 111. And so the first series of He 111A-0s carrying an armament of three machine-guns and a bomb load of 1,000 kg were exported to China. A total of ten of these machines were delivered. In addition, Heinkel also supplied China with a dive-bomber, the He 66, which closely resembled the He 50. One He 111A-0 was, however, kept back. Rebuilt and fitted with the new Daimler-Benz DB 600A power plants this machine was registered as He 111V5, D-APYS and in 1936 handed over to the Luftwaffe *Erprobungsstelle* (Test Centre) at Rechlin, the armament and bomb-load being the same as those of the A-0. Trials in Rechlin showed the He 111V5 to have a defect which turned out to be unfortunate: an over-compensation of the ailerons. This could, at certain speeds, result in the rudder action being reversed and, at low altitudes this could result in the total write-off of an aircraft. In Marienehe work was immediately put in hand to alter the wing-tips and the ailerons and cure the fault.

Although the He 111V5 did not have the required 400 km/hr (248·5 mph) speed, only reaching a maximum of 360 km/hr (224 mph) and a cruising speed of 340 km/hr (211 mph), the Luftwaffe were satisfied. An order was given for an advance series of ten He 111B-0s and four of these were sent to VB 88 in Spain.

Since the summer of 1936 German soldiers and airmen had been fighting for Franco. The fighting in the air had escalated with the intervention of the Soviet Union and French authorities that began to supply modern aircraft to the Republicans to combat Franco's insurgents. Against these a few He 51 biplane fighters and the improvised Ju 52 bombers stood little chance and an opportunity presented itself here to give operational trials to

Chief test pilot Gerhard Nitschke,
Prof Heinkel and Hayn, the Works ▼
Manager

▲ *Above and below:* The He 111V3, prototype for the
▼ He 111A-series, during its factory flight tests

▲ *Above:* One of the ten He 111A-1 bombers sold to China, with *(below)* representatives of the Chinese acceptance ▼ delegation

Right, top: He 111V5 in its original form as D-APYS and *(below)* the same aircraft as D-AJAK after all the modifications had been incorporated ▶

These were the first photographs of the new He 111B-1 bomber, released for publication in the British magazine *The Aeroplane*

48

KG 152 *Hindenburg,*
KG 153 *General Wever*
and KG 157 *Boelcke*
were among the first
units to be equipped
with the He 111B

Above: He 111Bs from the Norddeutsche Dornier-Werke (NDW) at Wismar ready for a factory test flight. *Centre:* An He 111B-2 taking off at Wismar

He 111B-1 *Werk Nr.* 1003 built by NDW, crashed on take-off at Bunzlau on an acceptance flight for the Askania automatic pilot installation. The date: 4 April 1936. The machine was flown by *Flugkapitän* Günther (co-pilot: Semrau)

View from one of the first He 111Bs crossing the Pyrenees on the way to Spain

The aircraft of the *Legion Condor* experimental bomber unit VB 88 were all known either as 'Pedro' or 'Pablo'; the He 111s were the 'Pedros'

VB 88 aircrews awaiting take-off orders

new bomber designs. An experimental bomber *Staffel* known as VB 88 was then set up under command of *Hauptmann* Rudolph von Moreau consisting of four each of Do 17E, Ju 86D and He 111B-0 bombers. In Moreau's old squadron all aircraft had been given the name of either 'Pedro' or 'Pablo' and the unit had become famous under the title of 'Pedros y Pablos'. VB 88 took over this tradition and, in addition, there were now 'Pedro I' and 'Pablo I' or, as the case might be, II, III or IV. When all modifications found by practical experience to be necessary had been incorporated an initial bulk order was given for 300 He 111B-1 bombers and delivery to the Luftwaffe began in January 1937.

Meanwhile VB 88 was undertaking its first mission in the Albacete sector where one He 111 was lost when hit in the fuel system by anti-aircraft fire. The crew were taken prisoner but later exchanged and returned home. The He 111B-1 differed from the B-0 mainly in the modification to its ailerons mentioned above, in having the more powerful DB 600Aa engines, improved radio equipment and an increased bomb-load of 1,500 kg (3,307 lb).

The first Luftwaffe unit in Germany to take delivery of the He 111B-1 was I/KG 154 at Fassberg (later KG 27 'Boelcke'). The first large-scale operational use of the He 111B was by VB 88 and K/88 on 31 March 1937 at 07.30 hrs when the assault started on the so-called 'Iron Ring' round Bilbao. During these battles a tragedy occurred which, even today, gives rise to controversy, the bombing raid on Guernica. *Generalmajor* Hugo Sperrle had ordered K/88 to effect the destruction of a road bridge being used by the enemy to transport troops and supplies into Bilbao. Visibility conditions were poor at the time of the attack and the He 111B-1 crews were not yet completely familiar with the new aircraft. Count Max Hoyos who was serving as a *Leutnant* at that time with VB 88 wrote: 'We went in with the new and complicated, but outstandingly practical and accurate bomb release-gear while the pilots accustomed themselves to the variable-pitch propellers and the aircraft's many innovations.' The bomb-sights, in particular, were at this time still comparatively primitive and even in 1940 during the Battle of Britain the bomber crews complained about the inadequacy of their sights. In short, the He 111 crews that attacked Guernica were still inexperienced and also had to contend with poor visibility and inadequate bomb-sights. As the smoke from the bomb bursts cleared following crews saw that the bridge had not been hit, but that the bombs had landed in the town in spite of the fact that strict orders had been issued not to attack the civilian population. Later, in their attacks on German cities and on Dresden in particular, both the British and the Americans bombed the civilian population on a massive scale as a matter of policy, but the raid on Guernica is still subject for heated discussions.

The performance statistics of the He 111B-1 series aircraft were as follows: cruising speed 345 km/hr (214 mph), operational ceiling 4,000 m (13,120 ft), range with full armament and a 1,500 kg (3,307 lb) bomb load 910 km (365 miles). At that time the only foreign bomber to better this performance was the Italian Savoia-Marchetti SM 79 powered by three engines totalling 3,000 hp to the He 111's 1,900 hp. The SM 79 had a cruising speed of 375 km/hr (233 mph), a range of 1,900 km (1,181 miles) and an operational ceiling of 6,500 m (21,320 ft). The defensive armament of the He 111B-1 consisted of three 7·9mm MG 15 machine guns. There was an Ikaria gun mounting in the nose and an open DL 15 mounting

Legion Condor

The He 111 *Kette* of
VB 88 on a sortie
over Spain

53

Pictures of He 111s in service with the *Legion Condor* in 1937/38.

Above: Bombing-up aided by willing Spanish ground staff.
Right and below: 'Pedros' over Republican territory

Left: After completion of operational trials with VB 88 the complete *Kampfgruppe* 88 was equipped with He 111B bombers. The two aircraft depicted above are from 2.*Staffel*/K 88

These He 111Bs of K 88 carry the insignia of I *Gruppe;* the same insignia was later adopted by I *Gruppe* of KG 53 *Legion Condor*

56

He 111B-1 in service as a trainer at Prague-Rusin (Rusyne) in 1940

He 111 as trainer

This He 111B lost its port wing tip after colliding with a Ju 52/3m at Prague-Rusyne on 2 November 1940

Another collision between an He 111B and a Ju 52/3m on 1 April 1941

Many crashes occured during training. This He 111B-2 belly-landed at Prague-Rusyne on 18 April 1940

The results of a collision between an He 111B and a Ju 52/3m on 20 April 1941.
Below: The He 111B GP + AR in turn had its tail unit damaged by another aircraft on 20 May 1941

The workshops at Prague-Rusyne had their work cut out to repair the damage to the aircraft in this crash, caused by defective undercarriage

The He 111B GP + AR, already damaged on 20 May 1941, tipped on its nose when landing on 17 November 1942, but apparently without any serious damage

with one MG 15 on the top of the fuselage. On the underside of the fuselage was a small retractable 'dustbin' turret, open to the rear and fitted with another flexible MG 15. For aerodynamic reasons the turret was kept so small that larger air-gunners had to hang their legs over the edge. With the amount of fighter opposition encountered over Spain this level of defensive armament proved quite sufficient but was to result in serious misconceptions that cost dearly later on.

The He 111B-1 was soon followed by the B-2 with more powerful DB 600CG fully super-charged engines developing 950 hp at critical altitude. This enabled the maximum speed to be increased to 370 km/hr (230 mph). The cooling system of the B-series was somewhat complicated. It consisted not only of large coolant radiators under the engines but, in addition to these, of two surface radiators either side of the engines and slightly aft of the leading edge of the wing. When the DB 600Ga with its improved cooling system was fitted into the later series models, the auxiliary wing radiators were discontinued.

Soon, Daimler-Benz could not keep up with the steadily mounting rate of airframe production and the question arose of finding an alternative power plant.

To this end a specially adapted He 111B-0 was used as a flying test-bed for suitable engines and designated He 111V6 (D-AXOH). The first engine to be tested was the Jumo 210, which only developed 640 hp and was, from the start, not powerful enough. Then, when the Jumo 211 became available, an intensive test programme was put in hand. These tests involved not only this engine but also the Junkers VS 5 variable-pitch propellers instead of the VDM propellers (VDM = Vereinigte Deutsche Metallwerke, Frankfurt-Heddern-

heim) which had been fitted with the Daimler-Benz power units.

Whilst this programme was still running, another He 111B-0 was modified to become the He 111V9, D-AQOX. This aircraft was the first with the DB 600Ga engines which, as already mentioned, had an improved cooling system enabling the auxiliary radiators to be discarded. The He 111V9 was intended as the prototype aircraft for a new He 111D-series. In the event only a very few He 111Ds were built because the Jumo 211 became available very quickly and the pressure could now come off Daimler-Benz, allowing them to concentrate on supplies for the fighter programme.

The continually expanding range of the He 111 programme made it necessary to introduce mass-production techniques which, at that time, were only in operation in the USA. Ernst Heinkel wrote: 'A whole area of the (Rostock) factory had to be equipped for series production of the He 111 and, what is more, for a type of series-production that had never until now been carried out, either in my works or even in Germany. With Works managers Paulus and later Hayn, two men whom I had just persuaded to come to Marienehe, I had to organize a system of assembly-line, conveyor-belt production . . . The whole production of the He 111 had to be divided into accurately-timed procedures. Production and transport of individual parts to the assembly line on which the aircraft to be built took shape required an extraordinary amount of carefully thought-out organisation: beginning with the fuselage, right up to the final assembly of the whole aircraft with engines, undercarriage, control surfaces and all the inside fittings being passed from team to team in intervals calculated exactly according to the time required for each process.' All this, which we now take for granted, had at that time to be developed from scratch. Already, by the end of 1936 and the beginning of 1937, the He 111 was being built not only in Marienehe but also under licence at the Norddeutsche Dornier-werke (NDW) in Wismar, the Allgemeine Transportgesellschaft (ATG) in Leipzig and at Arado in Babelsberg and Brandenburg/Havel and in subsidiaries of the Junkers works. Nevertheless, the production capacity was still insufficient.

The RLM urged Heinkel to build an even larger factory at Marienehe, but Heinkel did not want to involve himself too deeply financially. All his life he had been a businessman as well as a builder of aircraft. At this point *Generalmajor* Loeb, Head of the Luftwaffe Administration Office (LD), paid Heinkel a visit and put the suggestion to him that he should only lend his name and his experience to a factory that would be built by the German State. This new

Ernst Heinkel GmbH was to be established with an ordinary share capital of RM 5,000,000 with Heinkel himself receiving a RM 150,000 share. The only connection between Marienehe and the new works would be the production of the He 111 and the ultimate aim would be for a monthly output of 100 He 111s. Oranienburg in North Berlin was chosen as the location, primarily on account of its rail connections with Berlin. On 4 May 1936 the first trench was dug and exactly a year later, on 4 May 1937 the first He 111 was rolled out of the final assembly hall.

Although at this time the He 111 was continually giving proof of its efficiency in Spain, some problems continued to crop up. However, the aircraft themselves were not entirely at fault. At the NSDAP party rally in Nuremberg in 1937 three *Gruppen,* each consisting of twenty seven He 111s — coming from Crailsheim, Illesheim and Schwäbisch-Hall — were

The imposing entrance to the Heinkel Works at Oranienburg

Right: This photograph of an He 111D-1 in flight clearly shows the sky-blue undersurfaces in RLM 65 colour

Left: Heinkel He 111V6 D-AXOH was the flying test bed for the Jumo 211 engines intended for the He 111H series; it also featured a new type of gun mounting in the nose similar to that later installed in the H-10 series

Banking over the works' airfield this He 111D displays its 'splinter' camouflage of jagged grey, brown and green patches. The aircraft on the ground are two He 118 dive bomber prototypes

to take part in the Wehrmacht parade. Two days before the fly-past there was dismay at Marienehe. According to information received from *Oberstingenieur* (Colonel of Aeronautical Engineering branch) Lucht, the right-hand man of *Generalluftzeugmeister* (Chief of Aircraft Procurement) *Generalmajor* Ernst Udet, an He 111 had crashed for no apparent reason with wing failure. Heinkel sent Köhler, his colleague in many struggles, to investigate. He rang up next day to say that he had tested six wings and had found no fault, it must have been a case of pilot error. The following then came to light: when peeling off from close formation each pilot had to disengage from his neighbour and for this the aircraft had to put on a burst of speed. Now, the He 111, being comparatively large, was rather heavy on the elevator controls when accelerating at a steep angle of inclination and considerable physical effort was required of the pilot in order to bring the aircraft back onto the horizontal plane. The young pilots who had only recently completed their training had, in their inexperience and ignorance, tried to make things easier for themselves by making use of the trimming tabs which were not intended to be employed for straightening out and had thus placed too great a strain on the aircraft. Once Jupp Köhler had explained this to the pilots in minute detail the parade flight went off without a hitch.

After trials of the Jumo 211 in the He 111V6 had proved successful, one of the few He 111D-0s, D-ALEQ, was converted to a prototype for the new He 111E-series, the Jumo 211A-1 engines being installed, together with new retractable radiators and exhaust systems, and redesignated He 111V10. A small pre-production series of He 111E-0 bombers was completed immediately, corresponding to the V10 specifications with an increase in the bomb-load to 1,700 kg (3,748 lb), giving a take-off weight of 10,300 kg (22,707 lb).

At the end of 1937 the NDW in Wismar had established a production-line for assembling the He 111D-1 in tact method as evolved by Heinkel. Now, however, instructions were received from the RLM Technical Office (GL/C) to switch the He 111 production over to the Jumo 211-powered version, thus eliminating the D-series. From January 1938 onwards the first He 111E-1s came off the production-line, with specifications to a large extent similar to those of the E-0.

The squadrons of K 88 in Spain were re-equipped once more. VB 88 had been disbanded already in July 1937, having completed its task of trying out three new bomber types under operational conditions. Installation of the Jumo 211A-1 developing 960 hp had made it possible to increase the bomb load to 2,000 kg (4,410 lb) and the top speed to 390 km/hr (242 mph). An He 111E-2 series was dropped and so production on a large scale went ahead with the He 111E-3 with performance as detailed above and in 1938 this became the standard Luftwaffe bomber.

The He 111E-4 version which followed differed from the E-3 in that, in addition to the 1,000 kg (2,205 lb) internal bomb load a further 1,000 kg could be carried on external racks under the fuselage. However, only a short series of these was built. The same happened with the He 111E-5 long-distance version; this differed from the E-3 by having an additional fuel tank with a capacity of 835 litres (183·7 Imp gal) fitted into the fuselage.

The He 111 had also found other uses.

In 1937 Lufthansa handed two of its aircraft over to the Luftwaffe. These were the He 111V2, D-ALIX and the second He 111C-0, D-AXAV *Köln.*

Three views of the He 111D-1, of which only a few were built in late 1937 due to a shortfall in DB 600 engines which were earmarked for fighter production

Details shown in this cut-away of the He 111B are also largely typical of the He 111D and E series

Top and centre: He 111V10 D-ALEQ, a rebuilt He 111D-0, became a prototype for the E-series. *Below:* He 111V11 D-ARCG, a rebuilt He 111B-1, was used to test various wing forms ▶

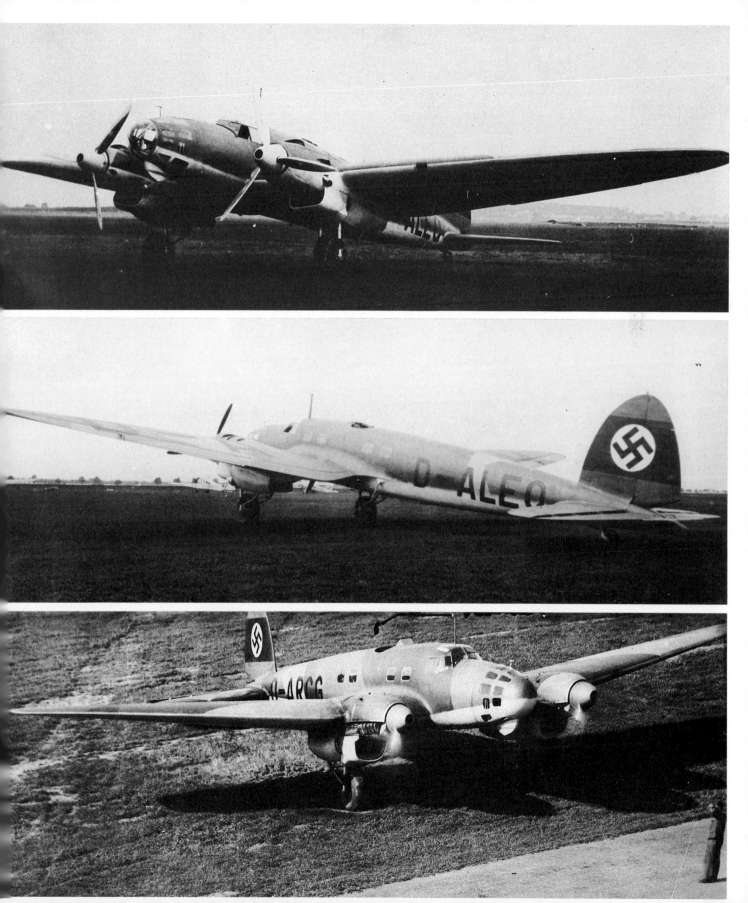

Production line of He 111E bombers built under licence by the Norddeutsche Dornier-Werke (NDW)

An NDW-built He 111E-1 taking off on a factory test flight

Some factory test flights had an unexpected ending, like this NDW-built He 111E-1

70

The He 111E-1 was also sent for operational trials in Spain with *Kampfgruppe* 88

In action with the *Legion
Condor:* He 111E, *Werk Nr.*
345, being bombed up

72

The carefree storage of bombs in completely uncamouflaged dumps clearly shows the command of the air enjoyed in 1938/39 by the Spanish Nationalists and their allies

73

The crew of an He 111E-1 of K 88 preparing for take-off. The same *Staffel* insignia was later used by 4./KG 53 *Legion Condor*

An He 111E from K 88 on an operational flight, with the gunner in the dorsal position keeping a careful lookout. *Below:* The bomb-aimer's view of the aircraft in front

75

The Standard of the *Legion Condor* at the farewell parade in Leon on 22 May 1939

The farewell parade in Leon. In the background are several He 111Es of III/K 88, with Henschel Hs 123 dive-bombers lined up behind

Above: He 111E-3 of KG 1 *Hindenburg* (ex-KG 152). *Below:* He 111E-3 56 + F12 after an undercarriage failure on landing in 1938

An He 111E-4 in service as a courier aircraft, with a Bf 108B Taifun in the background. *Below:* An He 111E-4 of FFS(B) 16 blind-flying training school at Burg near Magdeburg after its undercarriage had collapsed on landing

Some belly landings ended without much damage: an He 111E-3 at Königgratz on 27 June 1941. Others resulted in partial disintigration, like this He 111E TH + AI that swung around at the end of its landing skid in the same area ▶

This belly landing was not the end of He 111E DA + AZ ▶

On 16 July 1941 the repaired DA + AZ crashed into a farmhouse at Jenecz, killing and injuring several people

These aircraft joined a special, top secret Luftwaffe unit known as *Gruppe Rowehl* after its commanding officer *Oberstleutnant* Theodor Rowehl. This *Gruppe Rowehl* officially formed part of the RLM *Flugbereitschaft* (Flight Readiness Detachment) as *Fliegerstaffel z.b.V.* (Special Duties Flight), later becoming *Versuchsstelle für Höhenflug* (Experimental High-altitude Station) and finally *Aufklärungsgruppe Ob.d.L.* (Reconnaissance Group of the Luftwaffe High Command) and, before and during the war, carried out long-distance high-altitude reconnaissance flights. Initially they also used one or two He 70s, and became known later particularly in connection with the Ju 86P and R high-altitude reconnaissance bombers. The *Gruppe Rowehl* activities also show how early Hitler was contemplating war against the Soviet Union. The D-ALIX and D-AXAV were fitted with superchargers and hidden automatic cameras with lenses providing especially sharp definition and using infra-red film material. These two He 111Cs, still in their Lufthansa markings, flew on high-altitude photographic sorties over England, France and the Soviet Union as early as 1937. The flights over the Soviet Union extended as far afield as the Crimea and the Caucasus, distances only made possible by the installation of auxiliary fuel tanks. The modified He 111V2 D-ALIX crashed on one of these flights but, thanks to its excellent disguise, could be passed off as a civil aircraft that had lost its way.

In the meantime the He 111V16 had attracted interest in Turkey and the Turks bought four of these aircraft as the He 111G-5. This version was, in all respects, identical with the He 111V16 D-ASAR.

The He 111 continued to develop. The construction of the curved wing had given rise to production difficulties and Siegfried Günter was now working on designing a straight-edged wing that would have no aerodynamic drawbacks. Simultaneously and alone, since his brother's death, he was working on a new cockpit design, the step between the nose section and the pilot's cockpit having caused a certain loss of speed. To this end three new prototypes were built: He 111V11 (D-ARCG), in which different wing shapes were tested; He 111V8 (D-AQUO), with the old-type wings but with the first version of the new cockpit design; and, finally, the He 111V7 which already showed the characteristic outline of the He 111H- and P-series.

The He 111V11 had been converted from an He 111B-1 bomber and trials were carried out from July 1937 onwards with the new straight-edged wing shape which had to be modified several times: all armament mountings were improved and the *Plexiglas* dome at the nose section was replaced by a hemispherical sheet metal cone. This prototype was powered by DB 600CG engines but in all other respects it was identical with the D-1. The pre-production series of this version was built in 1937/38, the service trials were satisfactory and the production could go ahead. However, in the event only two short series were produced as the He 111F-1 with Jumo 211A-3 engines, a take-off weight of 11,000 kg (24,250 lb) and a range of 1,820 km (1,131 miles). A total of 24 machines of this version were built and released for export to Turkey.

The first aircraft left for Eskişehir on 19 October 1937. But the He 111F-1, D-AAAF, piloted by *Oberfeldwebel* Barte was unlucky. The machine, *Werk.Nr.* 5013, took off on 19 October from Oranienburg for the 1,333 km non-stop flight to Turkey, but it appears that something was wrong with the spark plugs of one of its engines necessitating an intermediate landing at Budapest. It was 22 October before D-AAAF could take off again to fly direct to Eskişehir via Belgrade, Sofia, and Istanbul. Since so much time had been lost, the planned landing at Istanbul for customs purposes had to be abandoned. In contrast to normal Luftwaffe colouring — black green/dark green upper surfaces with sky-blue undersurfaces — the Turkish He 111F-1s had their upper surfaces sprayed olive green.

In 1938 a series of 40 He 111F-4s were also produced for the Luftwaffe. These, apart from armament and equipment, were the same as the F-1 version. The bomb-load was split, as in the E-4 series: 1,000 kg were accommodated internally and 1,000 kg on two ETC 500 racks on the underside of the fuselage. But the most important change was that the F-series with the new wings had given the He 111 a new outline.

The first land-based German torpedo-bombers were also derived from the F-4. True enough, there were already such aircraft in the Luftwaffe inventory, such as the He 59 biplanes, but this was the first time that a fast, twin-engined land-aircraft was used in this role. The prototypes for this version, the He 111J, were the He 111V17, D-ACBH and V18, both of them converted He 111Bs. The He 111V18 was also notable for its identification markings: the civil registration that the earlier experimental machines and the first series-produced aircraft were given in the factory had in this case been altered by the insertion of the Luftwaffe cross e.g. as D-A+DUM (V18). Both these machines were used in trials of various torpedo carriers.

The He 111J-1 version was also powered by DB 600CG engines. The aircraft had two external racks enabling it to carry a 1,000 kg load. The LT F5b torpedo was jointly developed by the Torpedo Commission of the Navy under Admiral Gutjahr and the TLR/GL-E7 (Technical Air Armament) Division of the RLM and manufactured by the Torpedo Factory in Ahrensburg near Hamburg. A total of 90 of these He 111J-1 torpedo bombers were delivered to the Luftwaffe. They were later also used for laying magnetic mines. Subsequently, when the He 111H-6 went into service as a torpedo-bomber the remaining He 111J-1s were used for testing guided weapons and new types of aerial torpedoes. Thus, the Blohm & Voss L10 *Friedensengel* (Angel of Peace) glide-attachment designed to increase the distance from which the torpedoes could be launched, was tested with the He 111J-1. Before 1940 trials with aerial torpedoes were carried out at the Torpedo Experimental Establishment in Eckernförde and on the E-1 Torpedo Range at Leba in Pomerania. After the end of the Polish campaign, trials and tests were mainly carried out at the E-3 Torpedo Range at Hexengrund near Gotenhafen (now Gdynia).

In the autumn of 1938 the production of the He 111B, C, D, E, F, G and J versions at last came to an end and a new generation of He 111 bombers appeared. The strength returns of the Quartermaster-General of the Luftwaffe for 19 September 1938 show a combined force of 1,235 Do 17, Ju 86 and He 111 bombers, of which 1,019 were operational. The majority of the bomber units were, however, equipped with the He 111.

Total availability		Operational
He 111B	272	219
He 111E	171	141
He 111F	39	30
He 111J	88	78
Total	570	468 aircraft

Apart from its new wings the He 111F was basically an E-series airframe *Top:* He 111F-1. *Centre:* He 111F-1 supplied to Turkey. *Below:* He 111F-4, which led to the first Luftwaffe torpedo-bombers

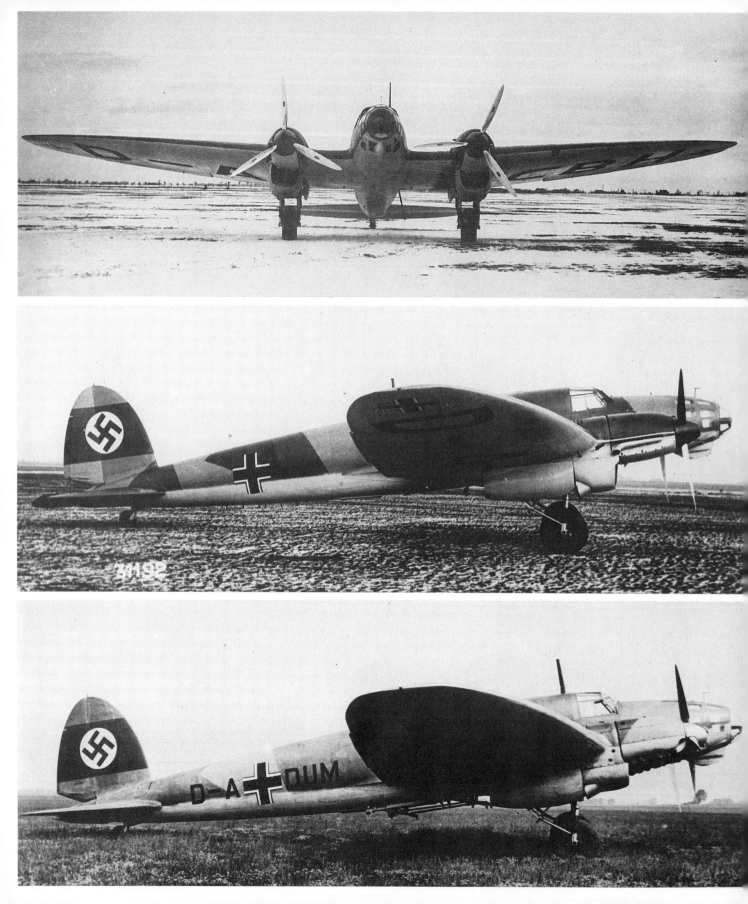

Left top and centre: He 111 V17 D-ACBH. *Below:* He 111 V18 D-A+DUM. These two machines were rebuilt He 111B airframes used to test various torpedo carriers

Crash landing due to defective port undercarriage of He 111 TN + AK at Prague on 12 November 1940

Küstenfliegergruppe (Kü.Fl.Gr.) 506 was the first unit to receive the He 111J-1 torpedo bombers. The subsequent amalgamation of this unit with Kü.Fl.Gr.306 resulted in *Kampfgruppe* (KGr.) 806, which in turn formed the nucleus of III/KG 53 *Legion Condor*

Centre and below: He 111J-1 bombers of KGr.806

86

He 111J-1 of KGr.806 over
the Pommeranian coast in
1939

Some He 111J-1s were later
used for trials with the Blohm
& Voss L 10 *Friedensengel*
torpedo-glider

87

Above: He 111J-1 with the L 10 *Friedensengel. Below:* An He 111J-1 used as a flying launch platform at an early stage in the A-4 (V-2) long-range rocket programme

A newly-completed He 111E at Rostock-Marienehe

General Ernst Udet, in charge of aircraft procurement and the Luftwaffe technical development, on a visit to the Heinkel works at Rostock-Marienehe

89

The He 111 gets a new look

As already mentioned, Siegfried Günter was working on a radical improvement of the He 111, compelled by several different reasons. The new wing design of the F-series, although easier to manufacture had less favourable aerodynamics, with a consequent loss of speed. Günter wanted to compensate for this by improving the outline of the fuselage and, in addition, the *Generalluftzeugmeister* or Chief of Aircraft Procurement (GL/C2) had been requested by the Luftwaffe High Command to insist on an improvement in the dorsal and ventral machine-gun positions in the He 111. The machine-gunner in the dorsal position *(B-Stand)* was exposed without protection to the slipstream and enemy fire, whereas the small, retractable turret *(C-Stand)* where the ventral gunner was located had repeatedly taken casualties from fighter attacks from behind and below during operations in Spain.

An He 111B-0, D-AQUO was then modified by having its original stepped forward fuselage replaced by one of entirely new design. Almost the whole of the crew space from the pilot's seat forward to the nose was glazed, the upper portion with curved panels and the lower with optically flat ones. In order to give the pilot the best uninterrupted view possible the nose machine-gun position *(A-Stand)* together with the bomb-aimer's position was shifted from the centre to starboard giving the

cockpit its typical assymmetric shape. The He 111V8, the end-product of these changes, made its maiden flight in January 1938. An He 111B-1, D-AHAY was modified (as V23) as the test aircraft for a new ventral machine-gun position. In its final form this took the shape of a long fairing combining a crew entry hatch and encompassing a prone gunner. In another He 111B-1, V7, a new dorsal machine-gun position was developed which was open to the rear but had a curved glass hood on the forward side.

The experience and test results gained through the He 111V7, V8 and V23 were then combined in the He 111V19, D-AUKY. The V7 resembled the V19 but was equipped with the new Daimler-Benz DB 601A engines of 1,050 hp rated power and became the prototype of the He 111P-series while the V19 became the prototype of the He 111H-series. The DB 601 fuel injection engine had been developed from the DB 600 by Dipl. Ing. Berger and Dipl. Ing. Nallinger of Daimler-Benz.

The He 111V7 had begun its trials already in summer 1938. The factory tests were followed by even more intensive trials at the Luftwaffe Test Centre at Rechlin, the German equivalent of the RAE, Farnborough. The Luftwaffe's assessment of the He 111P was most favourable and so, in the autumn of 1938, production of the P-series could begin and replace the He

111F and J-series on the assembly lines.

The new airframe was, from the beginning, designed to accept either of two different powerplants. The alternative engine was the Jumo 211 which had also been used in the He 111E and F-series. The first aircraft of the He 111P-0 pre-production series soon underwent service trials and the results were as good as those achieved at Rechlin. They were, in fact, so favourable that the RLM Supply Office (GL/E2) immediately increased their order for production aircraft.

The first He 111P-1s were delivered to operational units in the spring of 1939, and one of the first to receive them was KG 26, the 'Lion' *Geschwader,* commanded by *Oberst* Fuchs. The He 111V19 was also completed about this time and went for trials. This aircraft had the same airframe as the He 111P-1, but was powered by Jumo 211A engines with Junkers variable pitch propellers. Trials were as successful as those of the P-version and large-scale production of the H-series began at once. Heinkel works at Rostock-Marienehe and NDW at Wismar were primarily engaged in manufac-turing the He 111P whilst the He 111H was produced in Oranienburg, and also by Arado, Junkers and ATG.

Heinkel gave proof of what his talent for organisation could achieve. In the first nine months of 1939, up to the outbreak of war, a total of 800 He 111s were built. According to a strength return made on 2 September 1939 by the Quartermaster-General of the Luftwaffe the bomber arm possessed 1,197 Do 17, He 111 and Ju 88 bombers, of which 1,040 were operational. Just 18 of the new Ju 88 'wonder bombers' had been delivered and, in addition, there was a reserve of 30 Ju 86Gs. But almost 75% of bomber units were equipped with the He 111 as the following figures show:

Available aircraft		Operational
He 111E	38	32
He 111J	21	20
He 111P	349	295
He 111H	400	358
Total	808	705

Siegfried Günter with the wind tunnel model of the He 111 with the new fuselage

Above and below: The He 111V8 D-AQUO was a rebuilt B-0 airframe with a completely redesigned forward fuselage and the nose gunner's position offset to starboard. *Right:* The He 111V23 D-AHAY, a modified B-1, was used for tests with the ▶ new fully enclosed ventral gun position that replaced the old 'dustbin' type

The He 111H was to be built at Oranienburg while
production of the DB 601-powered He 111P-series was to
start in parallel at Rostock

Left: The He 111V19 D-AUKY combined the various improvements first tested on the He 111V8, V9 and V23 and was the
prototype for the Jumo 211-powered He 111H-series

The He 111J was still in use with *Küstenflie-gergruppe* (Kü.Fl.Gr.) 806 under Naval Aviation command. This unit later became *Kampfgruppe* (K.Gr.) 806 and was attached to 10 *Fliegerdivision.* The Ju 88A bombers appeared for the first time in the strength returns and equipped 1./KG 25 subordinated to *Luftflotte* 2. This unit was commanded by *Hauptmann* Pohle who, in June 1939, was still a Technical Staff Officer in the Operations Section of the Luftwaffe General Staff. In June 1939 Pohle had given an interesting lecture to the officers of the General Staff on the material side of the Luftwaffe armament. The following passages of this lecture are interesting insofar as they relate to the further development of the Luftwaffe during the Second World War. Pohle remarked that it had become apparent, as early as the autumn of 1937, that no German bomber had a penetration range of 1,000 km.

Since development of the big four-engined Ju 89 and Do 19 bombers had been discontinued as being unsatisfactory and no replacement was available, the existing medium-range bombers needed to be improved to meet this requirement and the Ju 88 put into production. The poor results achieved by bombers when attacking in level flight was another cause for concern. When attacking at high altitude in level flight it was apparent that bombing was only successful when areas such as large-scale industrial installations were the target, when bombs should be released in series. However, as in 1937 the Do 17 could only carry a bomb load of 250 kg (551 lb) it was unsuitable for stick-bombing attacks since bombs of less than 250 kg were ineffective. With just one 250 kg bomb on board each aircraft, little was achieved even by formation attacks. In contrast the He 111 was (in 1937) capable of carry-

Left: In the last months of peace the large-scale production of the He 111H and P-series went on under high pressure in both Heinkel factories; over 400 were delivered in four months

Below: The Luftwaffe airfields meanwhile presented a deceptively peaceful aspect. Sheep were often used to keep the grass short and even

The last stages in the assembly of an He 111P bomber

Three He 111Ps ready for their factory test flights

A massed fly-past of He 111s during Hitler's birthday parade on 20 April 1939

With such massed fly-pasts of Luftwaffe bombers Hitler sought to impress his allies and potential enemies. He is seen here with Prince Paul, the Prince Regent of Yugoslavia

Above and right: He 111P-1 bombers of KG 255 on training flights. *Left:* Another picture of the fly-past for Prince Paul

ing four 250 kg bombs but even a series of four bombs was not considered sufficient. The Ju 88 too could not perform much better than the new He 111P and H. Where high-level bombing was concerned, people would do well to remember Guernica: German bombers using this procedure had proved quite incapable of hitting pin-point military targets such as a bridge. But it was doubtful if the men who dropped the bombs really knew this themselves.

And it was with this qualitatively and quantitatively inadequate bomber force that the Luftwaffe entered the Second World War.

Baptism of Fire over Poland

Before the outbreak of the war the He 111 was hardly known to the German public, great emphasis having been laid on secrecy, but this was the case only in Germany itself. The attitude to the disemination of information overseas was however, considerably more generous and thus it was that the first pictures of the He 111B appeared, not in Germany, but in the British aviation magazine *The Aeroplane,* whose publisher, Mr C. G. Grey, had good relations with Ernst Udet, the Chief of Luftwaffe Aircraft Procurement. Apart from that through skilful use of propaganda the Luftwaffe was made to seem more powerful than it actually was, with mighty fleets of modern bombers.

Then came war. The Polish campaign had barely ended when two films appeared and were shown in all German cinemas. One was called *Feuertaufe* (Baptism of Fire) with an impressive musical score specially composed by Norbert Schulze, and the other *Kampfgeschwader Lützow.* So, quite apart from the newsreels where the photography was not particularly explicit, everyone now had a chance of seeing the He 111P and H. Particularly outstanding shots of the He 111 over Poland and the North Sea were shown in *Kampfgeschwader Lützow* and from this time onwards the He 111, alongside the Messerschmitt Bf 109 and the Ju 52, became one of the best known German military aircraft.

Delivery of the He 111P-2 with the FuG 10 instead of the FuG III had started in the summer of 1939 and this improvement in the radio equipment was also the only difference between these two versions. The flying schools received the He 111P-3, basically a modified P-1 with dual controls. The He 111H-1, in most respects similar to the pre-production He 111H-0 series, was delivered just before the outbreak of war, but the subsequent series did not leave the production lines until after the conclusion of hostilities in Poland.

The following Luftwaffe units were equipped with the He 111 during the Polish campaign:

Luftflotte 1 (*General der Flieger* Kesselring)
1 *Fliegerdivision* (*Generalleutnant* Grauert): KG 1; KG 26; KG 27
Luftwaffenkommando Ostpreussen (*Generalleutnant* Wimmer): KG 3
Luftwaffen-Lehrdivision (*Generalleutnant* Förster): Lehrgeschwader 1
Luftflotte 4 (*General der Flieger* Löhr):
2 *Fliegerdivision* (*Generalleutnant* (Loerzer): KG 4

In the *Luftflotte* 4 sector sixty He 111Ps of I and III *Gruppen* of KG 4 took off from Langenau in Silesia to attack Cracow, while II/KG 4

He 111 bombers of *Lehrgeschwader* (LG) 1 in readiness for the attack on Poland late in August 1939

The order for take-off has come, and crews run to their machines

An He 111H-1 taxies for take-off. The attack on Poland—and World War II—has begun

103

attacked Lvov. KG 4 had already been fully equipped with He 111P-2 bombers and their effect on the hangars and runways of the Polish airfields was devastating. In spite of this, the Polish Air Force, which was in its equipment inferior to the Luftwaffe, was not completely wiped out on the ground as expected. III/KG 4 under *Oberstleutnant* Evers flew in close formation, escorted by about 25 Bf 110Cs of I/ZG 76, and bombed according to schedule. As there was no sign of enemy fighters it was thought that the Polish Air Force had been knocked out; but this was not the case

and, in addition, the Polish anti-aircraft fire was very accurate. The Do 17s and Ju 87s frequently attacking at low-level suffered their first losses in this operation.

In the *Luftflotte* 1 sector, II *Gruppe* of *Lehrgeschwader* 1 (II/LG 1) attacked the airfield at Okecie near Warsaw where a strong force of Polish fighters was expected.

The He 111Ps took off that morning from Powunden in East Prussia in unfavourable weather conditions, but scored direct hits on their targets, notably on the *Panstwowe Zaklady Lotnicze* (PZL) aircraft factory, the largest

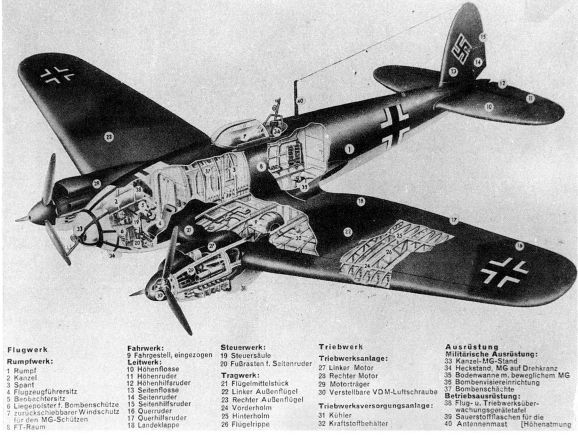

Flugwerk	Fahrwerk:	Steuerwerk:	Triebwerk	Ausrüstung
Rumpfwerk:	9 Fahrgestell, eingezogen	19 Steuersäule		**Militärische Ausrüstung:**
1 Rumpf	**Leitwerk:**	20 Fußrasten f. Seitenruder	**Triebwerksanlage:**	33 Kanzel-MG-Stand
2 Kanzel	10 Höhenflosse		27 Linker Motor	34 Heckstand, MG auf Drehkranz
3 Spant	11 Höhenruder	**Tragwerk:**	28 Rechter Motor	35 Bodenwanne m. beweglichem MG
4 Flugzeugführersitz	12 Höhenhilfsruder	21 Flügelmittelstück	29 Motorträger	36 Bombenvisiereinrichtung
5 Beobachtersitz	13 Seitenflosse	22 Linker Außenflügel	30 Verstellbare VDM-Luftschraube	37 Bombenschächte
6 Liegepolster f. Bombenschütze	14 Seitenruder	23 Rechter Außenflügel		**Betriebsausrüstung:**
7 zurückschiebbarer Windschutz	15 Seitenhilfsruder	24 Vorderholm	**Triebwerksversorgungsanlage:**	38 Flug- u. Triebwerksüber-
für den MG-Schützen	16 Querruder	25 Hinterholm	31 Kühler	wachungsgerätetafel
8 FT-Raum	17 Querhilfsruder	26 Flügelrippe	32 Kraftstoffbehälter	39 Sauerstoffflaschen für die
	18 Landeklappe			40 Antennenmast [Höhenatmung]

A partial cutaway drawing of the He 111P released in 1940. Most of the indicated parts are obvious, and include: 4. Pilot's seat 5. Observer's seat 6. Mattress for the bomb aimer 7. Sliding windscreen for the dorsal gunner 8. Radio operator's compartment 12. Elevator trim tabs 15. Rudder trim tabs 17. Aileron trim tabs 18. Landing flap 36. Bomb sight 37. Vertical bomb shafts 38. Instrument panel for flying and engine controls 39. Oxygen bottles

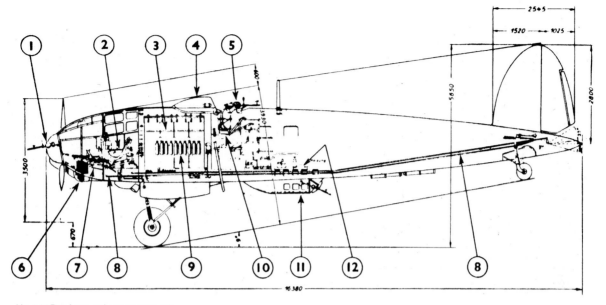

He 111P-1 internal arrangement

1. Forward flexible gun position (1 × 7·9 mm MG 15) 2. Pilot's seat 3. Vertical bomb magazine 4. Curved *Plexiglas* windscreen for the dorsal gunner 5. Dorsal flexible gun position (1 × 7·9 mm MG 15) 6. Lotfe *(Lotfernrohr)* telescopic bomb sight 7. Prone position for the bomb aimer and observer 8. Flight control push-pull rod linkage 9. Oxygen cylinders 10. Dorsal gunner's seat 11. Ventral flexible gun position (1 × 7·9 mm MG 15) 12. Heating installation

in Poland. KG 27 which should have followed it had to postpone take-off until 13.25 hrs because of bad weather. Also, their He 111s had a longer distance to travel since they came from Delmenhorst, Wunstorf and Hanover-Langenhagen. KG 27, in fact, belonged to the *Luftflotte* 2 sector (*General der Flieger* Felmy) and *Oberst* Behrends and his *Geschwader* had an approach flight of 700 km (435 miles). The He 111s, with an escort of Bf 110Cs from I(Z)/LG 1 did not reach Warsaw until 17.30 when the Polish Air Force made its first appearance in strength with about 30 PZL P.11c single-seat fighters. But the Polish early-warning system had not worked properly and the fighters did not take-off until the He 111s were over Okecie, five of them being shot down by the Bf 110s under command of *Hauptmann* Schleif who achieved one victory himself.

On 2 September *Oberst* Fiebig, *Kommodore* of KG 4, collected his whole *Geschwader* for a massed attack on the rail junction at Deblin. Deblin was about 56 miles south of Warsaw and had three airfields, none of which had been attacked the day before. The three formations flew at an altitude of about 4,000 m (13,120 ft) while, above them, a few of Bf 110Cs kept on the move in order to catch any Polish fighters that might appear. The bombers crossed the Vistula shortly after 10.00 hrs and the three *Gruppen* separated to attack the three airfields. The Polish anti-aircraft put up a furious barrage, but their range-finders appear however to have been inaccurate as all the anti-aircraft shells burst several hundred metres below the bombers, which were no more than jarred by the shock waves of the explosions. Runways, hangars and workshops were reduced to rubble and all that was left was a mass of craters. The escorting Bf 110s

105

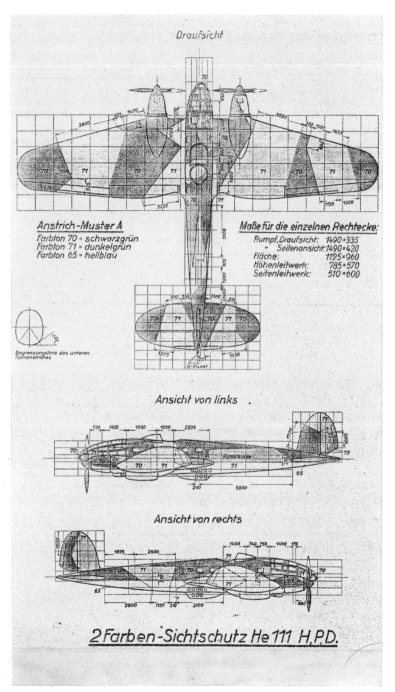

Draufsicht

Anstrich-Muster A
Farbton 70 = schwarzgrün
Farbton 71 = dunkelgrün
Farbton 65 = hellblau

Maße für die einzelnen Rechtecke:
Rumpf, Draufsicht: 1490×335
" Seitenansicht: 1490×420
Fläche: 1125×960
Höhenleitwerk: 785×570
Seitenleitwerk: 510×600

Begrenzungslinie des unteren
Tarnanstriches

Ansicht von links

Ansicht von rechts

2 Farben-Sichtschutz He 111 H.P.D.

106

discovered a few parked aircraft along the perimeter of the airfields and destroyed them in low-level attacks with gunfire. That evening the Wehrmacht communiqué announced that: 'It may be assumed that the Polish Air Force has been very severely crippled. The German Luftwaffe has won undisputed air-superiority over the whole Polish area.' This was not, in fact, true. The Poles had moved all their military aircraft to field airstrips where they had been carefully camouflaged. In spite of this however they were never able to regroup. Intensive German air attacks had destroyed most of the communications system, and the Poles were only able to fight on in desperation. There were also other forces standing by ready to fall on the carcase: on 17 September 1939 Soviet forces advanced into defeated Poland with two armies under Generals Kovalev and Timoshenko. The Polish Government fled to Romania and was interned there.

On 19 September Warsaw was surrounded and then subjected to a punishing bombardment. By this time the He 111 units had already been withdrawn and *Generalleutnant* von Richthofen, Commander of the VIII *Fliegerkorps,* who had been ordered to bomb Warsaw, had only Ju 87B dive bombers at his disposal and these could not drop incendiaries. Thus it was that Ju 52 transports dropped crate-loads of incendiaries from their side loading-hatches (without any attempt to aim) onto the already burning city — the film *Feuertaufe* shows this in detail. On 6 October the last Polish Army units surrendered and the campaign in Poland was over.

A pre-war RLM instruction sheet detailing the official two-colour camouflage scheme applicable to the He 111D, P and H

The Battle in the 'Watery Triangle'

One of the lessons to emerge from the campaign in Poland was recognition of the fact that the defensive armament of the He 111P and H, three MG 15s, was inadequate. The new He 111H-2 series was launched in the autumn of 1939, differing from the earlier H-1 by having more powerful engines and a heavier defensive armament: an additional MG 15 was incorporated in the nose and another into the ventral gondola. The engines installed were Jumo 211A-3s giving an extra 50 hp each. Crews sometimes even flew in their steel helmets since, as yet, the He 111 was unarmoured.

In the West the RAF had already made the first raids. In fact, the first bomb to fall on German soil was dropped on the night of 3/4 September 1939 on the little town of Heide in Holstein, probably by a Bristol Blenheim reconnaissance aircraft. The following afternoon came the first larger British bombing attack made by 10 Blenheims of Nos. 107 and 110 Squadrons on elements of the German fleet in the Schillig Roads and near Brunsbüttel. Three bombs dropped by the first five Blenheims actually hit the 'pocket battleship' *Admiral Scheer* but failed to explode. A short while later came another five bombers and the light cruiser *Emden* was severely damaged when a Blenheim of No. 107 Sqn, already ablaze after being hit by Flak fire, crashed and exploded on her forecastle. At about the same time fourteen Vickers Wellingtons, then the nucleus of RAF Bomber Command, attacked the battle cruisers *Scharnhorst* and *Gneisenau* off Brunsbüttel, but scored no hits. The first fighter kill of the Second World War was made on this occasion by *Feldwebel* Alfred Held of II/JG 77 (*Major* von Bülow). Altogether seven of the 24 attacking bombers were shot down.

Since the British had attacked first there should now have been a German retaliation. 10. *Fliegerdivision* had recently been formed for operations against Britain. This formation, which at that time only existed on paper, was commanded by *Generalleutnant* Hans Ferdinand Geisler, but at that particular point he had not a single aircraft at his disposal. It was not until the middle of September that KG 26, earmarked for the attack on Britain, returned from Poland. This unit consisted, however, only of two *Gruppen* and the *Geschwader* staff under *Oberst* Hans Siburg. Almost all members of KG 26 including *Generalleutnant* Hans Geisler, had originally served in the Navy. Admiral Raeder who commanded the *Kriegsmarine* had not been able to prevail against Göring and build up a Naval Air Arm like that of the US and Royal Navies: Göring maintained that everything that flew came under the Luftwaffe. During the course of the war it became evident how wrong this notion was since the

Luftwaffe and the *Kriegsmarine* never managed to reach a satisfactory degree of co-operation and later in the war during the Battle of the Atlantic, this was to have disastrous consequences for Germany.

Airmen who had formerly served in the Navy gritted their teeth and bowed to Göring's command, but strove continually to demonstrate in some fashion or another that they really belonged to the Navy. On one occasion the members of 10. *Fliegerdivision* even went so far as to have special caps made which differed from the Luftwaffe pattern. Göring was furious when he found out. He had promised Hitler to form thirteen *Geschwader* for the war at sea, but never fulfilled that undertaking. Thus it was that KG 26 was the only unit available for the battle against Britain — in actual fact, only two *Gruppen* of about 60 aircraft. In addition to this there were a few Ju 88A-1s of 1./KG 25 available under *Hauptmann* Pohle.

General Felmy, the Officer Commanding under whose command 10. *Fliegerdivision* came, was one of the group of officers, including Wilberg, Wimmer and Student (all of whom later became generals) who, before 1933 had secretly been building up a flying corps within the Reichswehr. When Göring took over and met these men and saw their work for the first time (previously he had had no contact with military aviation since 1919) he said: 'That was more than I expected!' It can safely be stated to-day that all the Nazi regime had to do was to step up production in order to turn the Luftwaffe into an effective weapon — all the development work had already been done.

Felmy and his Chief of Staff, *Oberst* Kammhuber, who later commanded the night fighters and became Inspector of the Luftwaffe in the post-war Bundeswehr, had no great opinion of the Ju 88 which, in any case, were pretty thin on the ground. He despatched I *Gruppe* of KG 26 to home bases at Hagenow-Land and Delmenhorst and had only kept four Ju 88As commanded by *Leutnant* Walter Storp in Westerland on Sylt. At this point there were only about 35 He 111Ps and 18 Ju 88A-1s operational. At 10.45 hrs on 26 September 1939 a Dornier Do 18D flying boat of *Küstenfliegerstaffel* 2./106 spotted a strong British naval force to the north of the Great Fisher Bank consisting of four capital ships and several cruisers. These were the aircraft carrier *Ark Royal* and the battleships *Nelson, Rodney* and *Renown* and the battle cruiser *Hood* — the strongest elements of the British Home Fleet. They were trying to lure the German Fleet out, but it wouldn't come. Instead Göring's 'Wonder Bomber', the Ju 88A-1, was sent to show what it could do. It turned out to be an absolute flop.

On direct orders from Göring who was particularly anxious for the Ju 88 to prove its worth, thereby justifying the enormous programme which had been put in hand for this bomber, Lt Storp was ordered to attack the fleet with the four Ju 88s under his command joined by a *Staffel* from KG 26. The Luftwaffe had made a considerable over-estimate of the effectiveness of dive bombing attacks on large warships. Storp chose the *Hood* as his target and scored a direct hit with at least one of his bombs, but had no luck: the bomb bounced off the deck armour and splashed into the sea. *Gefreiter* Dipl. Ing. Karl Francke, one of the most experienced test-pilots from Rechlin, was in another Ju 88 and attacked the *Ark Royal.* Two bombs fell into the sea close to the

He 111H-1 of KG 26 in a hangar and taking off ▶

108

Left: Two officers assist guiding a bomb being winched into the starboard fuselage magazine of an He 111P. *Right:* The flight engineer and the crew pet look out of the pilot's window. The KG 26 insignia is particularly clear

An He 111P of KG 26 in murky weather over the North Sea

The observer hands the pilot his flight combat rations. Normally, this would happen on the return flight

111

Inside the extensively
glazed nose of an
He 111H with the
observer prone
behind his MG/FF
cannon. Note the large
ammunition box and
the flexible
ammunition track

112

carrier but none of the pilots managed to get any clear picture of the effectiveness of the bombing because of the ships' devastating anti-aircraft fire. The He 111Ps were able to achieve nothing. But the next day Dr. Goebbels' propaganda machine announced the 'sinking' of the *Ark Royal.* In fact it was to be another three years before she actually was sunk — in the Mediterranean.

In the meantime 1./KG 25 had become I/KG 30 'Adlergeschwader'. KG 26 was entitled 'Löwengeschwader' because all the He 111s in the unit carried a shield on the fuselage nose section with a sitting lion and the motto: *Vestigium leonis* (The Lion's Footprint). I *Gruppe* had the shield in white, II in red and III in yellow.

On 8 October 1939 the German Fleet Commander Admiral Hermann Boehm in his flagship *Gneisenau* accompanied by the cruiser *Köln* and nine destroyers advanced along the Norwegian coast to a point off the Utsire Light. As expected, he was seen by an RAF Lockheed Hudson, a twin-engined reconnaissance aircraft, whereupon the British Home Fleet at once came out from Scapa Flow. Having achieved his object of enticing the British out, Boehm retired with his small force in the direction of the Skagerrak and Kattegat. At the same time KG 26 and I/KG 30 were alerted. It appears, however, that the German long-range reconnaissance was not functioning properly: most of the 127 He 111Ps and 21 Ju 88A-1s never found the British ships. Those few aircraft that did make contact attacked in level flight and did not manage to score a single hit.

The *Kriegsmarine* and Luftwaffe then began to use a new weapon to attack British shipping: mines laid by German destroyers and He 115 floatplanes along the east coast of Britain. Altogether 41 aerial mines were dropped by the Luftwaffe in three sorties — less than a tenth of what the Navy had laid in the same period.

Bad weather kept the He 111s of KG 26 largely inactive until the period between 17 and 19 December when they flew on what was known as 'armed reconnaissance', their task being to discover the movements of British ships and, where possible, to engage shipping targets. The crew of one of these aircraft, *Oberleutnant* Münter, *Oberfeldwebel* Moldenhauer, *Feldwebel* Lohel and *Feldwebel* Berden, became famous throughout the German press.

Their aircraft had been flying alone in the direction of the Orkneys and to be able to see anything had to fly just below the cloud ceiling, only a few hundred metres above the North Sea. A group of fishing vessels below them turned out to be neutral. The Heinkel also had a passenger on board, a radio officer making his briefing flight sitting between Münter, the observer, and Moldenhauer, the pilot. The radio operator occupied the dorsal gun position, the flight engineer the ventral position. Suddenly the radio operator shouted: 'Fighters!' simultaneously pressing the alarm button sending the strident sound of the alarm siren throughout the aircraft. The attackers were Bristol Blenheim IFs converted from an early series of Blenheim bombers to makeshift fighter-bombers and night fighters. The Germans defended themselves with their machine-guns as best they could against the three Blenheims. The radio-operator was grazed by a glancing shot on the forehead but continued undeterred to fire at the attackers. The flight engineer who could not fire at the attackers alongside, dragged his machine-gun from its mountings and rammed it through the side window firing on his adversaries from that position. By now the aircraft was jinking wildly, but not taking any evasive action. Something was obviously wrong. At last they managed to take shelter in the clouds and the radio-operator and flight mechanic left their posts to check what had happened. Then they saw exactly how hopeless their situation was. In the first British attack made from above, a burst of fire had smashed into the back of the pilot's seat. Münter saw Moldenhauer jerk and collapse, pulling the control column towards himself. He reacted quickly and, with the help of the radio officer hauled Moldenhauer out of his seat and himself slid into the pilot's position. As they did this, the aircraft twisted erratically, making it impossible for the British fighter to press home an attack effectively.

Münter himself had never piloted an aircraft before. The course on which they were heading was towards England and so he needed to fly in the opposite direction. He knew how to operate the rudder but had no idea that one also needed help from the ailerons and banked in a less than elegant fashion.

Moldenhauer had been hit three times in the chest dangerously near the heart. The radio-operator and radio officer bandaged him as best they could, using all the available bandages. The radio-operator now found that his set was not working. They were cut off from the outside world, and no one could help them. Münter continued to sit at the controls and reacted as best he could to the battering they received from the North Sea squalls, but in spite of all he could do the aircraft danced wildly above the waves. He put the aircraft into a steep climb up over the clouds trying desperately to get away from the storm but immediately had to come down again as the wings began to ice up. Then the engines started to make an ominous sound. Mol-

denhauer heard it, but could not speak and scrawled on a note-pad: 'Change the pitch of the propellers!' It worked, and the drone of the DB 601s returned to normal just as the pilot lost consciousness again.

After a three-hour flight the coast came into view. The observer had been able to establish roughly where they were and they even made it back to their own base. But what now? Should the inexperienced Münter risk trying to land? He wouldn't be able to bring it off. Moldenhauer couldn't speak but he was conscious again and had recognised the airfield. His eyes begged them to put him back into his seat, and hesitantly the observer and radio-operator obeyed the silent request. They had no choice! Within two minutes Moldenhauer had managed to bring the aircraft safely in to land before collapsing at the controls.

He recovered from his serious wounds. The whole crew were awarded the Iron Cross, lst Class and Moldenhauer, in addition, received a silver cup from Göring himself.

A heroic episode like this was a great morale booster, and naturally the well-organised propaganda machine made the most of it.

In the period between 17 and 19 December 1939 KG 26 attacked a British convoy near the Shetlands and succeeded in sinking some of the ships by bombing. They also made repeated attacks on other British shipping off the east coast of England. During these three days 10 ships totalling 2,949 gross register tons were sunk by KG 26, most of them fishing vessels, and a number of others were severely damaged.

The development of the He 111 took another step forward, thanks to experience gained in sorties over the North Sea. The next in the P-series to appear in 1940 was the He 111P-4, featuring heavier armament and armour pro-

114

Armed long-range reconnaissance over the North Sea late in 1939. *Below left:* The torpedoed British battleship HMS *Repulse* in dock at Rosyth photographed by an He 111 on 16 October 1939. *Right:* Lone long-range reconnaissance He 111 over the North Sea. These flights called for utmost vigilance, flying skill and stamina

tection. It was equipped with up to six MG 15s; 1,000 kg of bombs could be carried internally and a further 1,000 kg on ETC 500 racks on the underside of the fuselage. The augmented armament also brought an increase in crew from four to five. The last of the P-series which came out in 1940, was the He 111P-6. This had the more powerful DB 601N engines each developing 1,175 hp for take-off. The airframe was the same as the P-4, the total bomb-load of 2,000 kg being stowed in vertical *Elvemag* racks inside the fuselage. The protection for dorsal machine-gun position was improved and the defensive armament consisted of five MG 15s.

Some He 111P-6s were later equipped with *Rüstsatz* 2 (Standard Equipment set) as He 111P-6/R2 converting them into cargo glider tugs.

Early in 1940 the first aircraft of the large-scale He 111H-3 series left Oranienburg for delivery to operational units and from then on the H series replaced the P series which was being run down. This was because DB 601 engines were now required exclusively for fighter production, and from the end of 1940 only He 111Hs were built.

The He 111H-3 was born of the experience gained with the P-1, P-2 and H-1 and H-2 over Poland and the North Sea and was primarily intended for use against shipping targets. As well as its 2,000 kg bomb load the armament provided for attack and defence consisted of 20 mm MG/FF cannon in the forward section of the ventral gondola and an MG 15 in the after section; an MG 15 was mounted in the nose with another above it, the dorsal position had another MG 15, with a further MG 15 in each beam window. Protective armour had been improved, increasing take-off weight to 13,100 kg (28,880 lb).

From 9 to 30 January 1940 the He 111Ps of KG 26 continued to fly sorties attacking British shipping, and off the east coast of England they managed to sink twelve cargo ships and fishing vessels with a gross displacement of 23,944 tons and severely damaged a large number of others.

Then on 3 February 1940 Göring, in his capacity of Minister responsible for the Four Year Plan, sent a letter to Walter Funk, the Reich Minister for Economic Affairs, which proved to be one of the most decisive mistakes in German armaments policy. In this letter he said, among other things: 'During 1940 armament production must be pushed to the highest level possible. For this reason absolute priority is to be given to all projects capable of being completed by the spring of 1941. Should demands on production capacity make it necessary, all other programmes scheduled for later completion are to be postponed in favour of the above-mentioned intention.' This meant a complete ban on development work throughout the whole armaments industry, a ban which, in the years after 1942 was to prove so catastrophic for Germany.

At the beginning of March 1940 the Luftwaffe began to make attacks on British shipping in the English Channel. The first victim of these attacks flown by He 111s was a passenger ship sunk off the Isle of Wight. At the same time preparations were going ahead for Operation *Weserübung*, (Weser Exercise), the attack on Norway and Denmark.

Meanwhile something happened in February 1940 which clearly illustrates the lack of co-operation between the Luftwaffe and the *Kriegsmarine*. X *Fliegerkorps* under *Generalleutnant* Geisler had decided that the attack on British shipping was to be resumed on 22 February 1940. At 19.50 hrs on the day this decision had been passed to *Marinegruppe West,* and two *Staffeln* of KG 26 were ordered to attack merchant shipping in the area between the Orkneys and the mouth of the Thames. The He 111Ps took off in the morning of the 22nd, but bad weather forced them to turn back. At 17.54 hrs 4. *Staffel* of KG 26 took off again, having first informed *Marinegruppe West.* Among the aircraft was an He 111P, 1H+JM piloted by *Feldwebel* Jäger with *Unteroffizier* Schräpler as observer and bomb-aimer. This aircraft flew for about an hour on a northerly course, turned westwards over the southern tip of Sylt and then picked up the transmitter at Hörnum whose radio beam was to guide the He 111 on a bearing of 241° across the North Sea to the English coast. The radio-operator, *Unteroffizier* Schneider, was now responsible for the successful approach flight, the aircraft flying on at a cruising speed of 250 km/hr. About 19.20 hrs the flight engineer, *Unteroffizier* Döring, who was lying in the ventral gondola, reported streaks of white foam on the water. Shortly afterwards the observer also saw them.

Ships! The target they were looking for! As they had already overshot, *Feldwebel* Jäger turned left but hesitated to attack, since they had not yet reached their operational area. He banked over the target just as light anti-aircraft fire came up from below. This at least confirmed that the ships belonged to the enemy. The pilot pushed the aircraft down from 1,500 m and the observer kept a sharp lookout for the streak of foam. There it was! He released four 110 lb SC 50 bombs, of which only the third hit the forecastle of the ship below. Jäger decided to make another bombing run. It was now

19.45 hrs. He banked his Heinkel, levelled off and dropped a further four SC 50 bombs onto the shadowy form below. Schräpler, the observer, noted two hits amidships and then a column of flame. Immediately the whole ship burst into flames and began to sink. The time: 19.58 hrs. This at least is how the events appeared to the crew. What really happened?

Marinegruppe West had not informed X *Fliegerkorps* that six German destroyers were on the move and had been given the same task as the He 111s. The target that from above looked like a merchant ship was the last destroyer in the line, the *Leberecht Maass.* The second attack had scored hits not on this ship, but on the destroyer *Max Schultz.* Both ships sank with a loss of 578 lives. Hitler was furious. A thorough investigation by a commission from both services came to the conclusion that the basic reason for the disaster was that the aircrew had not been warned of the possibility of their coming across German warships.

Who was to blame? One thing is certain and that is that *Marinegruppe West* had received a clear signal at 12.18 hrs on 22 February informing them of the mission being flown by KG 26 and had done nothing about it. They had asked for air reconnaissance and fighter cover but had given X *Fliegerkorps* no information about the destroyers' mission. Admiral Raeder was forced to admit this tactical error in a report passed to Hitler on 15 March 1940. Four hours after the events on 22 February an He 111 flying in from the sea was shot down in flames by naval anti-aircraft fire. In this case, the question arises as to who had instructed the naval anti-aircraft gunners in aircraft recognition, since an He 111 was very easily recognisable.

Above left: A He 111H crew discussing their task shortly before take-off in winter 1939/40. *Right:* He 111H-3 of KG 26 in spring 1940. *Below:* A close formation of KG 26 He 111H-3s over the North Sea

Operation *Weserübung*

On the morning of 9 April 1940 the aircraft of three *Gruppen* of KG 4 based at Fassberg, Lüneburg and Perleberg and those of KG 26 at Lübeck-Blankensee and Marx in Oldenburg, all equipped with He 111Ps and Hs, were parked on the runways ready for take-off at the start of Operation *Weserübung*. KG 4 was at first primarily employed on propaganda missions over Denmark and Norway: just before 06.30 hrs one *Gruppe* of the *Geschwader* appeared over Copenhagen and dropped leaflets informing the population of the proposed German action and requesting to give up all resistance. III/KG 4 appeared over Kristiansand, Egersund, Stavanger and Bergen in a show of strength without dropping any bombs. Things did not go so smoothly for II/KG 4 over Oslo. Here was stationed a squadron of Norwegian Gloster Gladiators commanded by Capt Dahl. As the He 111s of KG 4 appeared over Oslo Fjord, where the burning wreck of the heavy cruiser *Blücher* already lay, the Gladiators immediately went in to the attack but the air-gunners on the Heinkels were able to defend their aircraft successfully. Other squadrons of KG 4 and KGr.100 (also equipped with the He 111H) dropped bombs on the airfield at Oslo-Kjeller, anti-aircraft positions near Holmenkol-len and coast defence batteries on the islands in Oslo Fjord. In the meantime long-range reconnaissance Do 17Ps of 1.(F)/122 had discovered that a strong British naval force (it was the greater part of the Home Fleet under Admiral Forbes) was approaching off Bergen. This was the moment that General Geisler, Commander of X *Fliegerkorps* who was directing the Luftwaffe operations during *Weserübung* had been waiting for. Just before midday 41 He 111Ps from KG 26 and 47 Ju 88A-1s from KG 30 fell on the British fleet in successive waves lasting for three hours. For the first time the Luftwaffe were able to attack the British fleet with telling effect: the battleship *Rodney* was hit by a 1,102 lb SC 500 bomb which, however, failed to penetrate the armour; the heavy cruisers *Devonshire*, *Southampton* and *Glasgow* were severely damaged, and the destroyer *Gurkha* sunk.

In the following period KG 4, 26 and 30 attacked the British and French troops that had been landed near Namsos and Andalsnes. Soon, however, both the He 111 *Geschwader* were withdrawn from the north as preparations had begun for the offensive against Holland, Belgium and France.

119

He 111H-3 bomber of KG 76 shortly before taking off on a sortie over Norway

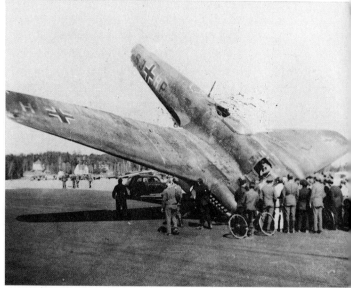

Above left: He 111H bombers and Ju 52/3m transports share the airfield at Oslo-Fornebu. *Above right:* This He 111H of KG 4 was shot down over Oslo-Fornebu by the Norwegian defenders. *Bottom right:* Another He 111 of KG 4 was forced to make a belly landing on the same airfield

This He 111 crashed at Björnefjell while operating in support of the German troops surrounded in Narvik

121

The Campaign in the West

In addition to KG 4, 26 and 30 that had been engaged in Norway, units fully or in part equipped with the He 111 participating in this campaign included *Kampfgeschwader* 1, 3, 27, 28, 53, 54 and 55 and KGr.100. The attack began on 10 May at 05.35 hrs; the night before, the entrances to the Dutch and Belgian harbours had been mined by He 115s. The most devastating surprise for the Dutch and the Belgians was the appearance at dawn of German bombers over their airfields. Albert Kesselring, commanding *Luftflotte* 2, had on his staff a specialist in night-flying who had put his crews through a tough training schedule of night take-offs, a squadron at a time. Crews often cursed this man who was continually driving them into the air in pitch darkness. The man in question was *Generalleutnant* Alfred Keller who had commanded *Bombengeschwader* 1 in the First World War. It was he who, with primitive equipment, had carried out the night bombing raids on Paris. After 1919 he became Director of Flying with the *Deutsche Luft-Reederei* and with Junkers-*Luftverkehr.* Then, however, when the Reichswehr began to create a flying corps in defiance of the Versailles ban he became Head of the German Civil Flying School (DVS) in Brunswick and there he trained the pilots who were to become the nucleus of the Luftwaffe after 1933.

KG 4 played a special role in the fighting in Holland. *Oberst* Fiebig, *Kommodore* of the *Geschwader* had already shown his special qualities during the Polish campaign; he was destined later to play a particularly tragic role at Stalingrad. The three *Gruppen* of KG 4 had taken off at 02.00 hrs from their airfields in Delmenhorst, Fassberg and Gütersloh. At 03.00 hrs the 28 He 111Hs of II/KG 4 appeared over Waalhaven airport in Rotterdam and dropped their incendiary and HE bombs on the target. Fiebig had led his group in in a wide sweep over the sea, hoping that by doing so he would take the Dutch by surprise. However, thanks to the treachery of General Oster in the High Command, the Dutch were aware of German intentions and KG 4 was received with furious anti-aircraft fire, added to which a number of Fokker D XXI fighters attacked the German raiders. Fiebig's He 111 was shot down, but he managed to parachute out and was taken prisoner — but not for long. The rest of his *Geschwader,* however, made a thorough job of it and all that was left of Waalhaven was a smoking, burning heap of rubble. It was here that 3 Battalion of the *Fallschirmjäger Rgt* 1 under *Hauptmann* Karl-Lothar Schultz dropped from their Ju 52s flown by III/KG.z.b.V.1. The battle for Rotterdam had started.

On 14 May when the tragic destruction of this famous old Dutch port occurred, capitulation plans were already under discussion. At the very time when the surrender of the Dutch defenders was being arranged, KG 54 commanded by *Oberst* Lackner equipped with He 111Hs had been ordered to attack Rotterdam. For technical reasons it turned out to be impossible to recall the force by radio and other aircraft managed to turn back only 43 He 111s while the remaining 57 aircraft dropped 97,000 kg (213,850 lb) of HE and incendiary bombs onto the city. The destruction was frightful and the toll included 900 killed and several hundred injured.

All the German Stuka- and *Kampfgruppen* were actively involved in the battles leading up to the break-through at Sedan and the rapid advance on Dunkirk. On 24 May *Panzergruppe Kleist* that had advanced to the line along the La Bassée Canal was halted on the advice of *Generaloberst* von Rundstedt, commanding Army Group A and on Hitler's orders 'in full agreement with him'. This order was given so that the armoured force could be preserved for Phase 2 of the French campaign and because it was thought that the low-lying polders of Flanders were unsuitable for armoured operations. In addition Göring declared arrogantly that the Luftwaffe on its own would wipe out the beleaguered enemy at Dunkirk, and ultimately this made the rescue of the British Expeditionary Force possible. On 26 May Anthony Eden, British Minister of War, ordered Lord Gort, C-in-C of the British troops in France, to withdraw on Dunkirk while the British Admiralty made emergency preparations for their evacuation. This operation codenamed 'Dynamo' began on 27 May 1940. The Luftwaffe meanwhile tried its utmost to fulfill Göring's pledge, the attacks by German Stukas and bombers exceeding even the worst British expectations.

The attacks began at dawn on 27 May. First to appear were small groups of He 111 bombers from KG 1 and KG 4. The flashes of exploding bombs lit up the darkness joined by the flickers of the first fires. The stream of bombers never stopped, and then He 111s from KG 54 dropped incendiaries onto Dunkirk docks. Alongside the long Eastern Mole the 8,000 ton French freighter *Aden* broke apart under hits from HE bombs. These level attacks by units of *Luftflotte* 2 lasted until 07.11 hours.

They were followed by Stukas from VIII *Fliegerkorps,* and then came Do 17Zs from KG 2 and 3. Now however RAF fighters flying from bases in Southern England appeared in the air and the bombers and Stukas began to take losses. Then German fighters joined the fray and wheeling dog-fights took place over the beaches of Dunkirk. Off shore, ship lay close alongside ship, and many were sunk or set on fire — but nothing could stop the evacuation of the bulk of the British troops: 'Operation Dynamo' saved a total of 338,226 men. All that remained behind was the BEF's heavy equipment and about 40,000 French troops who had covered the retreat and had then been left behind by the British. At the end of 'Operation Dynamo' on 4 June only 15% of British troops had been either killed or captured. But the whole of the British Army's equipment was lost and, on top of that, there was the loss of shipping: altogether 272 ships were destroyed off Dunkirk, nine of them destroyers. With the collapse in the West there was no other course for the Allies but to withdraw from Norway.

On 3 June German bombers, to a large extent He 111s, attacked the French air industry, mainly concentrated in the outskirts of Paris. Aircraft and engine works were hit with HE and incendiary bombs crippling a major part of the French air armament industry. When two days later the Battle of France

The forward-facing MG 15 in the ventral gun position

An SC 250 bomb being winched up into the vertical fuselage bomb magazine

A close-up of the Jumo 211D-1 engine fitted on the He 111H-3

124

He 111P-2 of KG 55, the *Greifengeschwader,* taxiing for take-off

proper began, units of *Luftflotten* 2 and 3 supported the Army's advance with successive waves of attacks on French troop concentrations. The French capitulation took place on 22 June 1940.

A Control Commission was set up to oversee compliance with the cease-fire conditions and for this purpose some He 111Hs and Ps were converted to communications aircraft. Several of these aircraft were discovered by the Allies later in French North Africa as, for example, D-APOW in Oran, and D-ACLQ in Algiers.

Another He 111 used by this Commission was registered D-ARAJ.

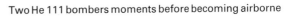

Two He 111 bombers moments before becoming airborne

Right: He 111 bombers on the way to their 'lightning victories' in the west

He 111H-3 bombers during the French campaign. *Left:* Posing before the take-off *(centre)* A newly-delivered replacement machine, still without armament and *(bottom)* In low-level flight in search of enemy armour

54356

He 111H-2 T5 + AU of
*Aufkl.Gruppe des
Oberbefehlshabers
der Luftwaffe,* or
Gruppe Rowehl, in
winter 1939/40

The same aircraft
taking off from
Oranienburg

128

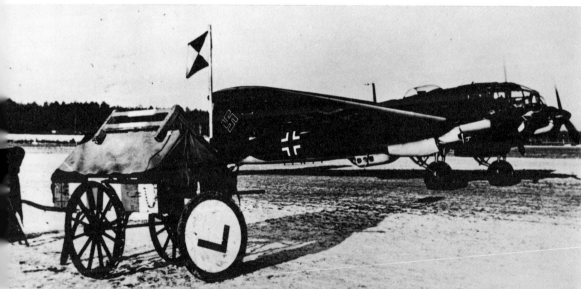

Three more pictures of He 111H-2 aircraft from *Gruppe Rowehl.* The overpainted factory delivery code letters HP + MO are still discernible on T5 + BU *(bottom)*

129

From top to bottom:
Preparations for the
next sortie being
carried out on an
He 111P-2 of KG 27
Boelcke; He 111P of
KG 27 at Köthen
before the attack on
France; He 111s of KG
27 flying westwards

Right, top to bottom:
He 111P-6 G1 + LT of
KG 55; an He 111 shot
down over France; an
He 111H-3 of KG 27 in
summer 1940 ▶

Two He 111 bombers (He 111P and H) converted into communications aircraft for the German Armistice Commission in France

The Battle of Britain

The first He 111s appeared over the British coast on 18 and 19 June 1940 and bombed harbour installations. And on 10 July, for the first time, larger forces from *Luftflotten* 2 and 3 bombed military targets in the South of England. The British count this date as the start of 'The Battle of Britain' which, again according to British reckoning, lasted until 31 October 1940.

According to Directive No. 16 issued by Hitler on 16 July preparations were to be made for a landing operation 'if necessary'. Directive No. 17 followed on 1 August with the order that 'intensified sea and air operations against Great Britain be undertaken'. The intensified air-war against Britain first ordered only on 1 August, began with the so called *Adlertag* on 13 August 1940 and did not end, for all practical purposes, until the Luftwaffe units were withdrawn from the West in 1941 to take part in Operation *Barbarossa,* the attack on the Soviet Union.

Between 10 July and 13 August, attacks were only made on British convoys in the Channel in the course of which intervention by fighter units from both sides led to dog-fights. During July the Luftwaffe sank 40 Allied merchant ships totalling 75,698 gross tons and four British destroyers in the Channel. In a discussion with *Grossadmiral* Raeder, Hitler suggested 15 September as the day to be appointed for an invasion of England. The final date was, however, not to be fixed until after eight days' intensified air offensive. Subsequently, a further discussion took place with the Commander-in-Chief of the Army, *Generalfeldmarschall* von Brauchitsch and his Chief of Staff *Generaloberst* Halder in which Hitler announced his decision to attack the Soviet Union in the spring of 1941.

The following He 111 units meanwhile were alerted for the intensified air offensive against Britain:

X *Fliegerkorps*	KG 26
I *Fliegerkorps*	KG 1 (in part already with Ju 88A)
II *Fliegerkorps*	KG 53
9 *Fliegerdivision*	KG 4 (in part already with Ju 88A)
V *Fliegerkorps*	KG 55
IV *Fliegerkorps*	KG 27

The two last-named units belonged to *Luftflotte* 3; the others, with the exception of X *Fliegerkorps,* to *Luftflotte* 2.

The He 111P-4s of KG 4 opened the battle with intensive mine-laying operations in the Thames and Humber estuaries and the harbour entrances of Penzance, Plymouth, Liverpool, Southampton, Falmouth and Belfast with magnetic mines, lasting from 8 to 12 August. Then came 13 August, 'Eagle Day'. The

An He 111 prepares to take off for a
night raid on Britain, autumn 1940

weather however upset all calculations and only 485 bomber and about 1,000 fighter sorties were flown on this one day, after which the attacks were continued mainly at night. The mine-laying aircraft from KG 4 and almost all other He 111 units were in the air.

A particularly successful raid was the bombing of the Nuffield Works in Castle Bromwich manufacturing Spitfires. On 15 August the Luftwaffe flew 2,119 sorties particularly directed at airfields in the South of England with a loss of 55 German aircraft. On 16 August, a total of 1,720 German aircraft were in action over England and in the days that followed the attacks continued to concentrate on RAF airfields. However, it seems that the German Intelligence had not done its work properly and, in addition had probably misinterpreted the evidence of long-range reconnaissance. The bombers seemed to have a scant idea of the location of their most dangerous enemies, the RAF's Spitfires and Hurricanes, or of where fighter aircraft were being built. There were no intensive attacks either on the airfields of Fighter Command or on the factories producing fighters.

In the period between 22 and 25 August, X Fliegerkorps mine-layers were busy again, mostly He 111s from KG 4, laying mines at the harbour entrances of Dundee, Newcastle, Middlesbrough, Hartlepool, Dover, Portland, Poole, Scapa, the Thames estuary and the area round the Isle of Wight. Meanwhile KG 26 subordinated to Luftflotte 5 had suffered heavy losses. On one occasion British radar had picked up He 111s flying in from Norway at a distance of 160 km (99 miles) from the coast with the result that the Heinkels (at this stage without their Bf 110 escorts) came under continuous attack from Nos. 41, 79, 605 and 607 Squadrons and were unable to carry out their

tasks. Eight He 111s, almost 10% of the force, were shot down. Then on the night of 24/25 August something happened which was to divert the course of the war in the air into dramatic new channels.

Rochester and the Thames docks were among the targets set that night, but something went wrong with the navigation of the He 111s detailed for this task. Ten aircraft found themselves over London itself, the capital city whose bombing Hitler had strictly forbidden. Several bombs were dropped, and damage inflicted. The result was an order from Churchill for an attack on Berlin. Immediately Hitler gave the go-ahead for London to be bombed.

Luftflotte 3, including KG 27 and 55 were ordered only to attack at night. Naturally, this meant a certain amount of adjustment for crews who had been used only to daylight operations. For this reason KGr.100 equipped with He 111H-3s with a reduced bomb-load but improved radio equipment were detailed to act as 'Pathfinders'.

The continuous attacks on their airfields were having such a punishing effect on RAF Fighter Command that even the bomber crews were beginning to notice. One He 111 crew of II/KG 1 'Hindenburg' reported 'only slight fighter activity which was successfully held off by the escort (JG 52, 53, 54)'. On the night of 25/26 August came RAF Bomber Command's riposte to the supposed attack on London on the night of 24/25 August: 81 Hampden and Wellington bombers took off to raid Berlin, and 29 reached the target. On the night of 28/29 August there was another raid on Berlin and a third the following night. On 2 September mines were again laid in the approaches to some British harbours and estuaries. Following this on the night of 5/6 September came the first heavy night raid on London carried out by Luftflotte 2,

Right: Propaganda shots of He 111 ▶ bomber formations flying to attack Britain

An He 111P being pushed back into its revetment after a raid

He 111H-1 of KG 26

An He 111H approaches to land while another taxies out for take-off

the main target being dock installations in the Port of London. A total of 60,000 kg (132,270 lb) of HE and incendiary bombs were dropped which started four extensive and four smaller fires. The RAF replied at once with a raid on Berlin the following night.

On the German side Operation *Loge* (Theatre Box) started on 7 September, being a series of raids on London which would last for 65 days. Hitler's decision to switch the weight of the attack away from the fighter airfields onto London however, the very moment when Fighter Command was near breaking point was the saving of Great Britain. Winston Churchill himself conceded this in his memoirs. It was one of the many catastrophic strategic decisions made by Hitler in the Second World War.

In the night raids on Britain it had become apparent that the bombers, mainly He 111s, experienced few difficulties in their attacks on London since they could get their bearings from the meandering course of the Thames that glinted in the moonlight. When attacking other targets however they had more problems in the dark. But here they had recourse to the *Knickebein* navigation system that had been developed by Dr. Plendl at Rechlin. This device was used for the first time in the notorious raid on Coventry on 14 November 1940. Two squadrons of He 111H-3s from KGr.100 fitted with this equipment 'rode' along a guidance beam emanating from the *Knickebein* transmitter on the French coast and accurately directed in a straight line onto Coventry. The pilot corrected his course according to signals received on a radio set: dots and dashes in his headphones informed him whether or not he was straying from the beam, a continuous tone told him that he was on course. In the meantime the wireless operator was waiting at the

second *X-Gerät* receiver for the 'preliminary signal' given by a second beam intersecting the main beam at an angle. When this signal sounded the aircraft was only about 20 km from the target and the wireless operator now only had to press the button starting the X-clock. The next ten kilometres served as a calibrating distance to determine the true speed of the He 111 over the ground. At the end of this 10 kilometre stretch the aircraft entered a third guidance beam and the 'main signal' was heard. The button on the X-clock was pressed again: the first hand remained stationary while the second continued to run. At this point the pilot had to stick exactly to the prescribed speed, course and height. As soon as the second hand on the dial reached the first the bomb-release switch made contact and the bombs automatically left their bays and external racks. The 18 He 111H-3s from KGr.100 reached Coventry on the dot and the first fires started up below them—the target was marked. Following them came about 450 bombers of *Luftflotten* 2 and 3, most of them He 111Ps and Hs and they dropped 50,300 kg (110,890 lb) of HE and 881 incendiary clusters onto Coventry. By the standards of 1940 the effect was fearful: 554 dead and 965 badly injured, not to mention the material damage. It must, however, be noted that Coventry was a major centre of the British armaments industry and therefore a legitimate target.

None of the following attacks on other cities reached the intensity of this raid. The deterioration of the weather as winter deepened forced the raids to slacken off. Another mine-laying offensive took place between 12 and 19 December, the weather being particularly suitable for such operations, and 300 mines were dropped claiming 12 ships totalling 20,675 gross tons. London was twice severely bombed between Christmas 1940 and the new year. Hitler, however, was by now almost exclusively preoccupied with preparations for campaign against the Soviet Union; there was no longer any talk of an invasion of England.

In the meantime the re-equipment of German bomber units with the Ju 88 was in full swing. The Do 17 and the Do 215 were phased out and long-range reconnaissance was also increasingly going over to Ju 88Ds. Even some of the *Kampfgeschwader* that had only flown the He 111 such as, for example, KG 54, were re-equipped with the Ju 88. The crews were not too pleased about this, as the robustness, reliability and, not least, the He 111's good-natured behaviour in the air had made it popular. For this reason quite a few bomber units remained faithful to the He 111, all the more so because the Ju 88 programme was still not progressing as it should have done. Back in Rostock-Marienehe the opinion was that the possibilities of the He 111 had by no means been exhausted and that its performance could be improved still further. Günter and Schwärzler worked untiringly at improving the aircraft.

Some of these developments, though, were not so successful, as for instance the He 111H-8. In the raids on Britain barrage balloons had proved to be effective counters to bombers and thus a barrage balloon deflector was devised and mounted on the He 111H-3. Thirty modified aircraft were delivered but showed such unfavourable flight characteristics that they were withdrawn after the first losses over Britain. The order for them was cancelled and the cumbersome 'Balloon Deflector' framework *(Rüstsatz Mg)* with its electric cutters (code-named *Klettenmagazin*) which had made the aircraft nose-heavy was dismantled. Later in the war the remaining aircraft redesig-

nated He 111H-8/R2 were used for towing cargo-gliders.

At the beginning of 1941 a new version, the He 111H-4 was produced but, in spite of its versatility only a short series was built. The H-4 was fitted with the improved Jumo 211D-1 and later also H-1 engines. The fuselage bomb-load was kept at 1,000 kg but the external ETC racks were replaced by PVC racks which could carry a 1,800 kg (3,970 lb) load. This made it possible to transport externally either the SC 1000, SC 1800, SD 1400, SD 1700, SB 1800 type bomb or the PC 1000, PC 1400 and PC 1600 armour-piercing bomb. When carrying a reduced bomb-load of 1,000 kg the He 111H-4 could also be used on longer-ranging operations when fitted with two extra PVC 300 litre (66 Imp.gal) fuel containers and an additional 835 litre (183·7 Imp.gal) fuel tank in the fuselage giving it a range of over 3,000 km (1,864 miles).

A report in the Luftwaffe magazine *Der Adler* of 11 February 1941 shows the kind of treatment an He 111 could survive. This report accompanied a picture of an He 111 that had made a belly-landing with the following caption: 'An outstanding achievement! On the return flight this Heinkel He 111 was attacked by a large number of enemy fighters. Despite this the German aircraft continued on its course and landed having sustained 700 hits.' The report said nothing about the condition of the crew who must probably all have been more or less seriously wounded, or how exceptional this case really was.

The He 111H-4 was followed by the H-5 with the same armament as the H-3 and H-4 but with a bomb/fuel load increased to 4,550 kg (10,030 lb). Half of the bomb load was normally carried internally and half on the external PVC racks. The He 111H-5 was powered by Jumo

Another two propaganda shots taken at the Rechlin Test Centre showing simulated attacks by a captured Spitfire fighter

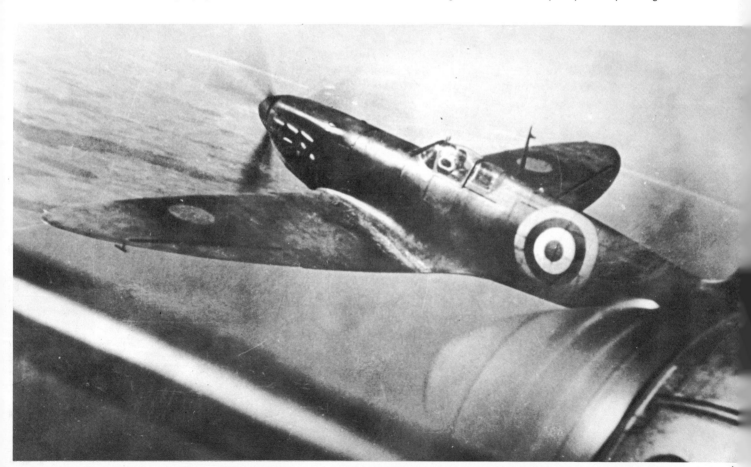

A genuine—and famous—photograph showing an He 111 over a bend of the Thames in London

211D-1 engines with VDM variable pitch propellers. Again, only a small series was built.

The new year of 1941 was 'opened' by *Luftflotte* 3 on the night of 2/3 January with an attack on Cardiff by 111 He 111Hs in which 115,000 kg (253,530 lb) of HE and 292 incendiary clusters were dropped. The following night Bristol was the target and on the night after that it was Avonmouth. On the night of 9/10 January it was the turn of Manchester and London and the following night London alone was the target. The pressure on Britain was kept on.

The He 111H-8 was a development that did not work. Intended for barging aside and cutting the cables of British barrage balloons, these contraptions made the aircraft unwieldy and slow. The few machines that survived these hazardous operations were later converted for glider towing

Two He 111P-2s of KG 55 over Britain. Note the blotched undersurfaces and half overpainted wing crosses of the upper machine, and the insignia on the rudder of the lower He 111

Wreckage of an He 111 shot down over a British airfield

143

This He 111P of KG 26 just managed to reach the North Sea coast where it made a belly landing

Another crew look ruefully at their aircraft while the film cameraman records the combat damage. This He 111P-2 too made it back once more, but only just

Concentration shows on the face of the He 111 pilot: he knows that the fate of his crew largely depends on his skill

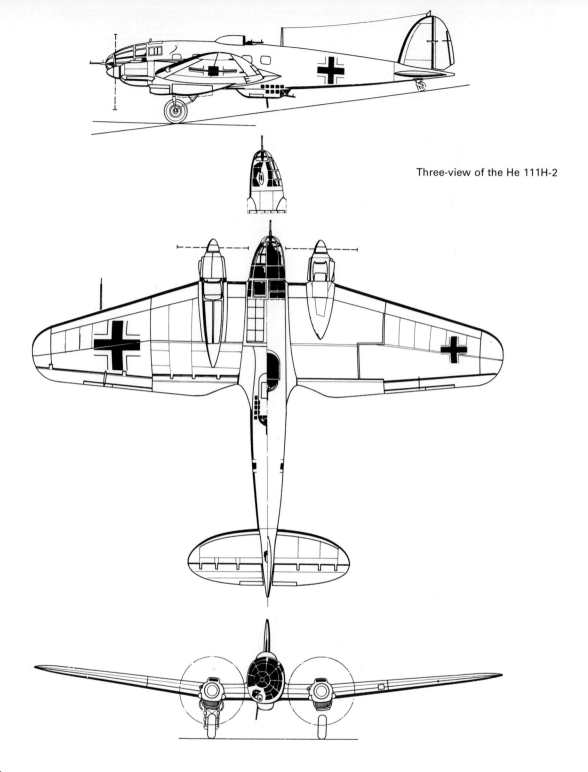

Three-view of the He 111H-2

146

This He 111H-1 fell almost intact into British hands in February 1940 when it was forced down with a dead crew member after an interception by a Spitfire. Subsequently repaired, it was repainted in British camouflage colours (apart from the KG 26 insignia) and allocated the RAF serial AW 177. As part of No. 1426 (Enemy Aircraft) Flight this He 111H was used for demonstration and fighter training purposes until 10 November 1943 when it stalled on take-off. Of the ten men aboard seven, including the pilot Flg.Off. F. A. Barr, were killed. This captured He 111H is seen here in flight and with an FW 190A-3 and Ju 88A-5 of No. 1426 Flight

Crew of an He 111. *Left:* The pilot,
(right) the radio operator, and
(below) the bomb
aimer/observer/nose gunner, all in
one

148

Two He 111H bombers of KG 53 *Legion Condor* shortly after take-off

A bad collision after landing. This He 111 of KG 53 is painted entirely black for night operations. Note the obliterated white edges of the fuselage cross

The insignia of 4.*Staffel*/KG 53 *Legion Condor*

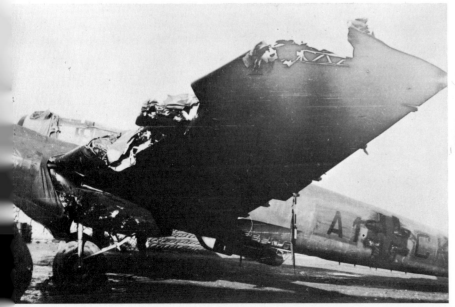

149

Top: He 111H-3 of KG 26 running up its engines, with the pilot waving from his open escape hatch. *Right:* An original individual insignia on an He 111H of KG 27

◀ *Left, top to bottom:* He 111H-3 GA + MJ before delivery to an operational unit; He 111P-4 bombers on an airfield in France. A captured French light tank (minus its turret) has been impressed to tow the aircraft; He 111H in the winter of 1940/41 on another French airfield

Above: The crew of an He 111 going out to their aircraft for another raid. *Below:* This He 111H of KG 26 belly-landed on the French coast with the last drops of fuel

Above: This is the way the attacking He 111 formations made their way across the Channel. *Below:* And this is how they would often end up after an encounter with RAF fighters

The Mediterranean and the Balkans

Meanwhile, in the Mediterranean the position of Germany's Italian allies was becoming critical. Cyrenaica had been lost and the Italian Fleet was continually being harried by the Royal Air Force and the Royal Navy. The attack on Greece had been thrown back into Albania and Mussolini begged Hitler for help. Then came the fall of Prince Paul, the Regent of Yugoslavia, and defiance from the new rulers in Belgrade. As a result Hitler was forced to postpone the attack on the Soviet Union and secure his southern flank. One of the measures taken was the formation of the *Afrika Korps* (DAK) under *Generalleutnant* Erwin Rommel and the despatch of the first German units to North Africa to bolster the flagging Italians. At the same time X *Fliegerkorps* under *Generalleutnant* Geisler was moved to Sicily. During the week 6 to 13 January it sank the heavy cruiser *Southampton* and badly damaged the aircraft carrier *Illustrious*. On 16 March two He 111H-4s converted to torpedo-bombers flew an armed reconnaissance sortie in the area around Crete and, to the west of the island discovered a British naval force consisting of a number of battleships, cruisers and destroyers. Both crews, members of KG 26 torpedo *Staffel,* chose the most important targets and attacked the battleships. In spite of furious anti-aircraft fire they dropped down to 250 m and flew to within almost 1,500 m (1,640 yds) of the ships before releasing their torpedoes. As they turned away they could just see columns of water at the ships' side and were firmly convinced that they had scored hits, reporting this on their return. As the reports of both crews tallied, *Generalleutnant* Geisler had no hesitation in passing this information on to the Italian Naval Command and this was to have dire results. The Italians considered the British force to have been sufficiently weakened by the loss of their heavier units and felt able to risk an attack. The result was the naval battle off Cape Matapan which resulted in an annihilating defeat for the Italians. The British had a weapon which the Italians did not possess: radar! The British battleships, with the help of their radar, could 'see' their adversaries clearly in the night battle that developed whilst the Italians were virtually blind. They lost two cruisers and two destroyers and the battleship *Vittorio Veneto* was badly damaged by torpedoes.

In the meantime the air raids on Britain continued to a more limited extent. Up to 31 March British civilian losses had been 6,131 killed and 6,900 wounded.

The German assault on Yugoslavia and Greece began on 6 April 1941. No He 111 bomber units were involved in this campaign and, the aircraft engaged in the North African theatre of war were mostly Ju 87 and Ju 88s, the He 111 still being mainly occupied in bombing British targets. At the beginning of

May 1941 they carried out a series of five night attacks on the Liverpool-Birkenhead docks sinking 18 merchant ships totalling 35,605 gross tons and damaged a further 25 totalling 929,964 gross tons. The dock installations were so extensively destroyed that the harbour's turn-round capacity was reduced by 75%.

In April Germany received support from an unhoped-for direction in the Near East, support whose value Hitler failed to appreciate—he had always under-estimated the importance of the Mediterranean area—and he failed to make proper use of the chance offered. The Arabs, who felt that they had been betrayed by Britain at the end of the First World War, emboldened by Rommel's successes, hoped for German support for an attack on British strategic bases in the Near East. The Iraqi government under Ahmed Ghailani surrounded the British base as Habbaniyah with troops and asked Hitler for armed help against the British. Instead of supporting the Iraqis in strength, with an eye to their oil supplies, the only help sent was a small 'special detachment' consisting of a mere six He 111H-3s and three Bf110Cs under *Oberst* Werner Junck who had been a fighter leader with *Luftflotte* 3 during the Battle of Britain.

This small unit landed at Damascus and Palmyra on 12 May and flew on to Mosul on 14 May. The British soon found out about the German aircraft and attacked. As early as 15 May some Blenheim V bombers from Habbaniyah raided Mosul, destroying one He 111 and two of the Bf 110s. Junck ordered a counterattack and the remaining He 111H-3 of his detachment flew a total of six bombing and seven reconnaissance sorties. In the meantime II *Gruppe* of KG 4 had been moved to the Mediterranean area. On the night of 17/18 May they flew from Sicily to North Africa and, after a refuelling stop, continued in the direction of Egypt. Almost unnoticed, they managed to penetrate as far as the Suez Canal and dropped 45 mines into the navigating waters totally blocking the canal for some considerable time.

No He 111 units were engaged in the German landings in Crete which took place between 20 May and 1 June. On 31 May Junck's force had to abandon their mission in Iraq for want of supplies and support from home. The aircraft, which in the meantime had been given Iraqi markings, were by then for the most part no longer airworthy and were left behind. A single He 111 brought home the remaining personnel, the majority having already been repatriated via Aleppo and Rhodes, and an important opportunity had been lost. Hitler was only interested in war against the Soviet Union. In June twelve armoured divisions and twelve motorised divisions were transferred to the east and the concentration of the Luftwaffe against the Soviet Union began on 10 June. Almost all units were recalled from the west, leaving behind only two fighter *Geschwader* and three or four bomber *Gruppen* along with a few long-range reconnaissance aircraft. The whole force that the Luftwaffe could muster was now concentrated on the Eastern Front and in the Mediterranean area. Operation *Barbarossa,* the attack on the Soviet Union, began on 22 June 1941 at 0315 hours.

The He 111H-4 was the first version to have an external PVC bomb rack under the port side of the fuselage

Ground crews of several He 111s assist in attaching a heavy bomb on the PVC rack

He 111H-4 with an SC 500 bomb. Only the starboard internal bomb magazine was retained

He 111H-3 featured an 20 mm MG/FF cannon in the ventral gun position

Left and below: It is generally though that the He 111H-6 was the first torpedo carrier of the H-series, but in actual fact it was the H-4. Shown here are LT F5b practice torpedoes with red-white noses on PVC racks

157

The torpedoes had to be dropped at the right speed and height to ensure success, and the crews trained accordingly. Laden with practice torpedoes, an He 111H-4 taxies out on a training flight

The torpedo-bomber levels off and the first torpedo is released

The He 111 becomes the 'Maid of all Work'

It is only when one considers the length of the front along which the concentration took place (about 6,000 km or 3,728 miles from Finland to Romania), that the low strength at which the Luftwaffe embarked on Operation *Barbarossa* can be appreciated. According to the establishment of the units involved, 1,945 aircraft were assembled. The actual strength, that is the number of aircraft that were operational, amounted to only 1,280—about two thirds of establishment. The breakdown was 510 bombers, 290 dive-bombers, 440 fighters, 40 twin-engined fighters and 120 long-range reconnaissance aircraft. In addition, it must be borne in mind that the aircraft were, to a large extent, already obsolescent, since the Ju 87s and the Bf 110s, i.e. the Stukas and *Zerstörer,* had had to be withdrawn as early as 1940 from operations against Britain: they could no longer be used in the West.

The following bomber units were still equipped with the He 111:

Luftflotte 4 (*Generaloberst* Löhr)
V *Fliegerkorps* (*Ritter* von Greim)KG 55 'Greif'
IV *Fliegerkorps* (Pflugbeil   KG 27 'Boelcke'
Luftflotte 2 (*Generalfeldmarschall* Kesselring)
II *Fliegerkorps* (Loerzer)KG 53 'Legion Condor'

By the summer of 1941 the He 111 had already been largely replaced by the Ju 88, but was still an aircraft of some importance. In fact, the ageing bomber could not be easily dispensed with, as it was capable of performing a number of tasks for which the Ju 88 was unsuited. Shortly before the start of the Russian campaign some He 111 *Geschwader* had been equipped with a new modification of this bomber which, like the He 111H-3, was also to be produced in large numbers—the He 111H-6. This version was powered by an improved version of the Jumo 211, the F-1 series with the Junkers variable pitch propeller that could be recognised by its broad blades with their light-weight wooden casing. In other respects the He 111H-6 was very like the H-5 which was distinguished by the narrow-bladed VDM airscrews. As with the H-3 and H-5, the armament consisted of five MG 15s and one MG/FF.

The MG/FF cannon was a weapon 'with a history': it was a licence-built version of the Swiss 20 mm Oerlikon cannon which, in turn, was an improved version of the 20 mm Becker cannon developed as an aircraft gun in Germany in 1917/18. As early as 1918 this weapon was fitted into the Hansa-Brandenburg W33 monoplane flying-boat and the AEG G IVK bomber. In 1918 the cannon disappeared from Germany and reappeared after the war in Switzerland. Thus Germany was manufacturing a German weapon under licence.

The first aircraft of the He 111H-5 series. All offensive loads were carried externally on two PVC racks ▶

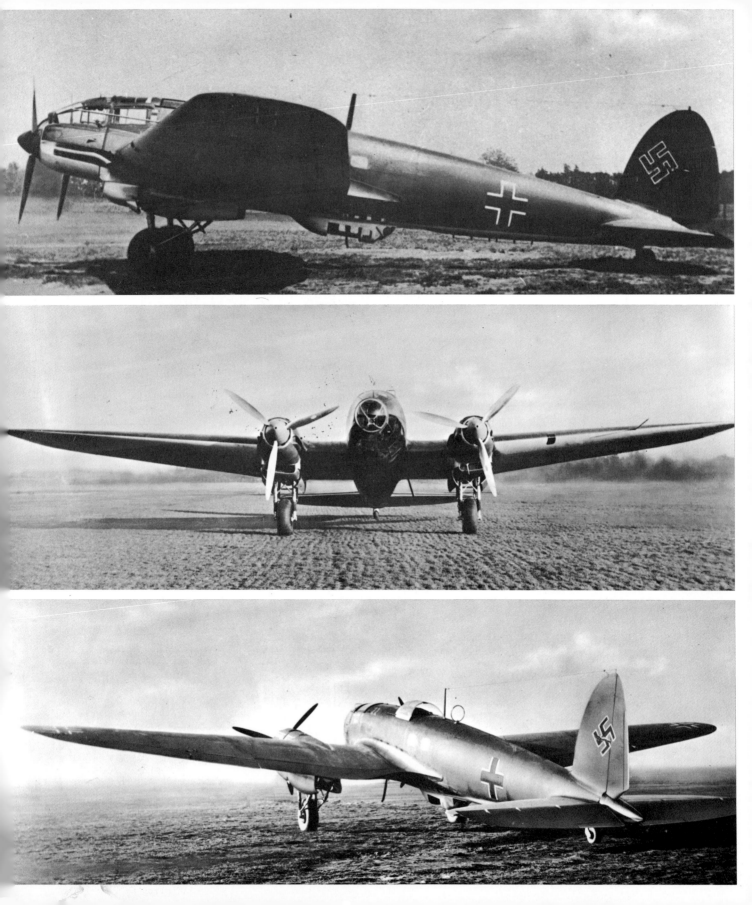

Above left: An He 111H-5 flying over the predictor of the airfield Flak battery. *Right:* He 111H-5 of KG 76

Left: An He 111H-5 parked beside a FW 56 Stösser aerobatic trainer at the *Luftkriegsakademie* Gatow (air warfare academy), Berlin

Right, top: He 111H-2 NG+ JQ communications aircraft at Palermo in 1941. *Centre:* He 111H-5 destined for Romania before delivery, and *(below)* in Romanian air force service on the Eastern Front

Left: One of the few He 111H-5 bombers used in the West under camouflage netting

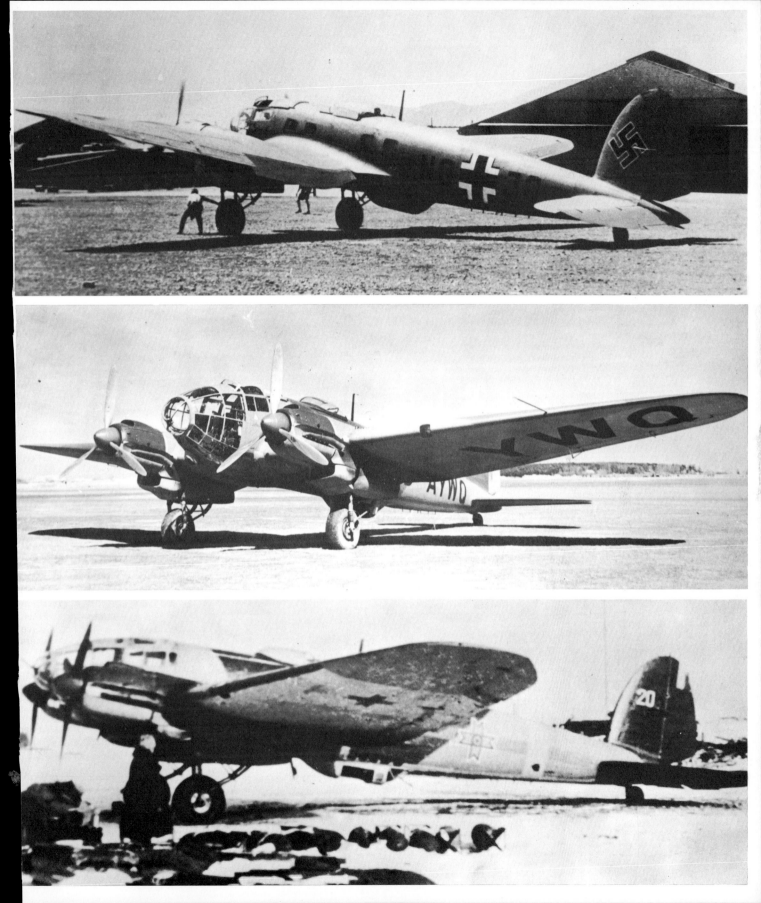

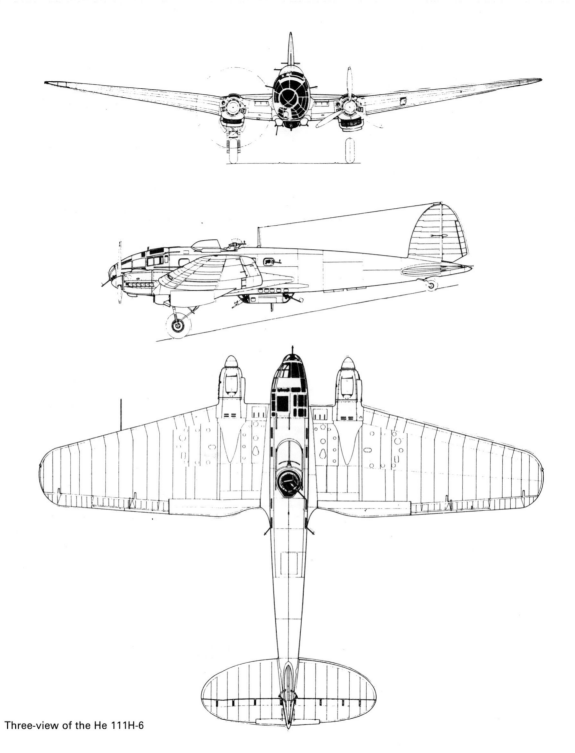

Three-view of the He 111H-6

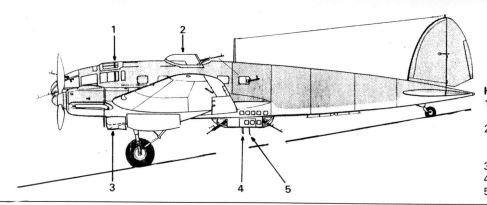

He 111H-3

1. Sliding roof for pilot's emergency exit
2. Forward-sliding curved windscreen for the dorsal gunner
3. Semi-retractable radiators
4. Trailing aerial
5. Rod aerial

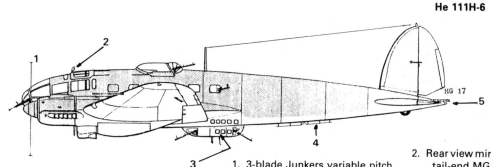

He 111H-6

1. 3-blade Junkers variable pitch propellers (He 111H-5: 3-blade VDM variable pitch propellers)

2. Rear view mirror to aim the fixed tail-end MG 17
3. Crew entry hatch
4. Dipole aerial for blind landing

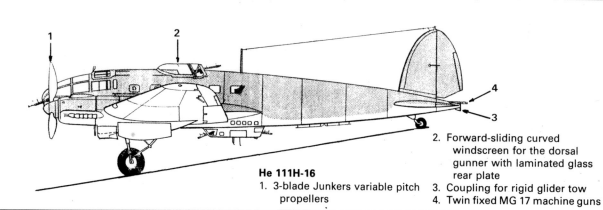

He 111H-16

1. 3-blade Junkers variable pitch propellers

2. Forward-sliding curved windscreen for the dorsal gunner with laminated glass rear plate
3. Coupling for rigid glider tow
4. Twin fixed MG 17 machine guns

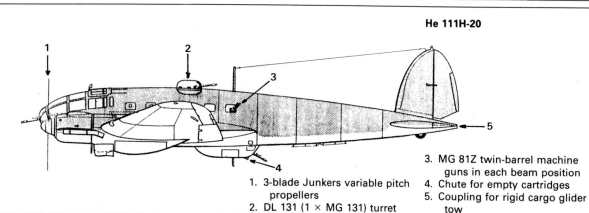

He 111H-20

1. 3-blade Junkers variable pitch propellers
2. DL 131 (1 × MG 131) turret

3. MG 81Z twin-barrel machine guns in each beam position
4. Chute for empty cartridges
5. Coupling for rigid cargo glider tow

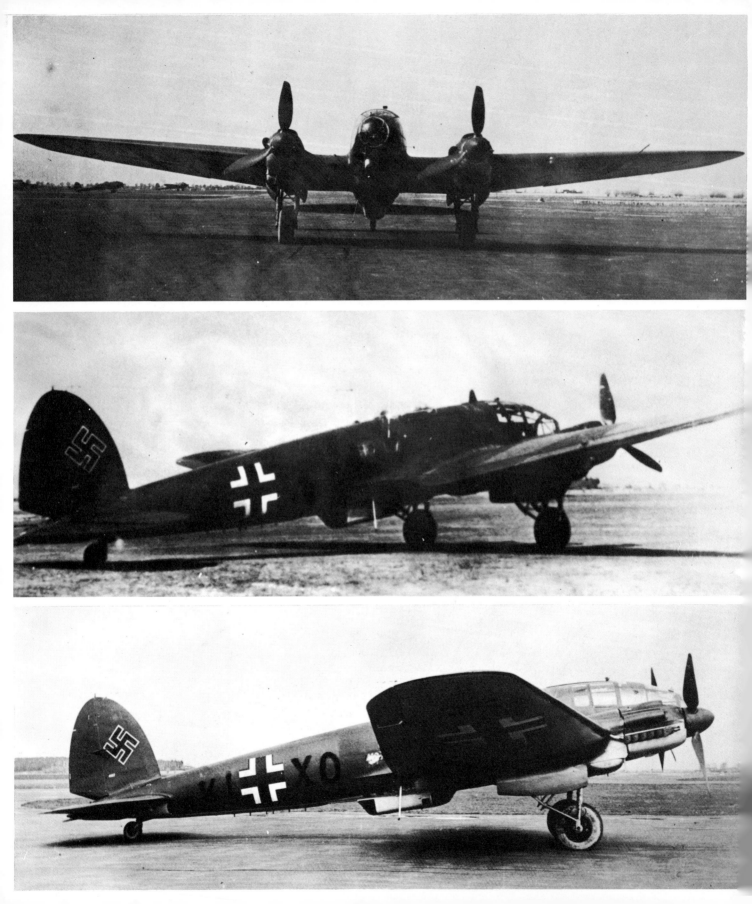

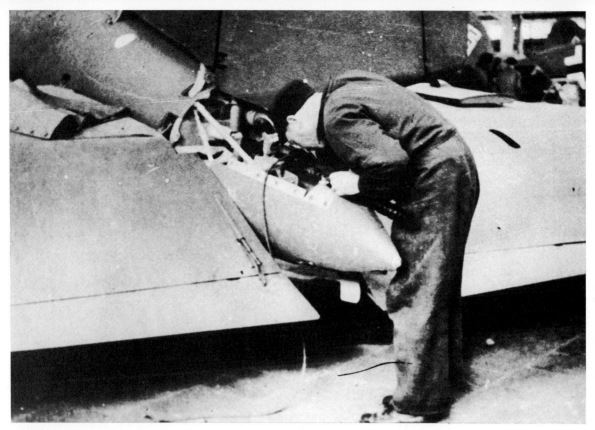

◀ *Left:* The main external difference between the He 111H-6, which was produced in large numbers, and the H-5 lay in the wide-bladed Junkers variable pitch propellers; the He 111H-5 had narrow-bladed VDM propellers

As a particular sting in the tail for fighters attacking from the rear the He 111H-6 was fitted with a fixed MG 17 in the fuselage tail cone. It was aimed and fired by the pilot via a spacial rear-view mirror

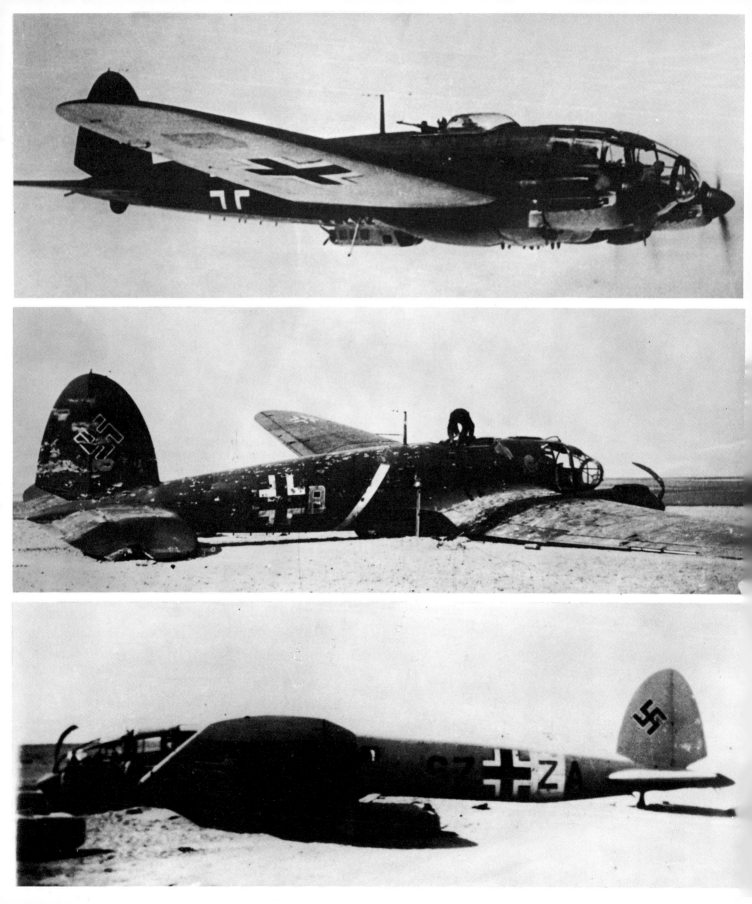

Left top: He 111H-6 in flight. *Centre:* An He 111H-5 shot down by Soviet fighters. *Bottom:* He 111H-5 used as communications aircraft by *Stab/Stukageschwader* 3 (Stab/St.G.3) blown up by own troops before the German retreat in North Africa

Right: This He 111H got safely home despite being badly shot up. *Below:* An He 111H-6 of KG 26 at Derna, North Africa, on 15 June 1941

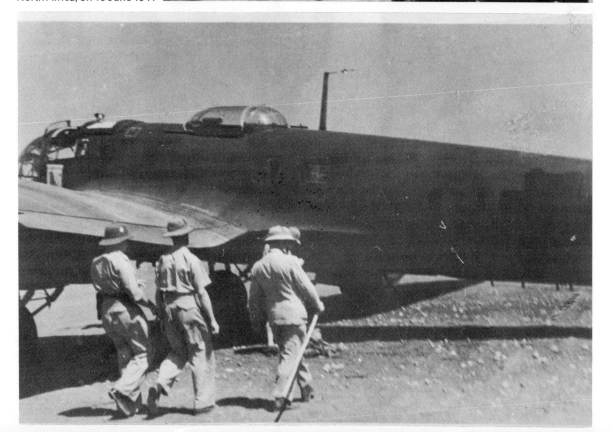

The He 111H-6, however, possessed yet another additional weapon against attack from behind which could not be seen by the radio-operator from the dorsal position because of the rudder unit: a fixed MG 17 built into the fuselage tail cone. This gun too could be fired from the dorsal position. As with the preceding models, the H-6 carried a crew of five and a bomb load of up to 2,500 kg (5,512 lb). It could, at will, be quickly converted for use either as a bomber, mine-layer or torpedo aircraft and proved its worth in all these capacities for a long time under active service conditions.

On the night of 11/12 July He 111H-6s from KG 4 successfully attacked the port installations of Port Said and Ismailia on the Suez Canal causing fires and damage to the port installations. Since no British night fighters were stationed there all aircraft returned to their bases undamaged.

On 8 July Hitler announced his decision to raze Moscow and Leningrad to the ground. However, as the Luftwaffe failed to attack the capital on account of the continual demands made on them by the Army for air support, Hitler expressed the opinion to Göring at the OKW (High Command of the Armed Forces) that the Luftwaffe had lost its nerve. Whereupon all available bomber units were rustled up and co-operation with the ground forces came temporarily to an end.

The first raid on Moscow took place on the night of 21/22 July and all available He 111s from KG 27, 53 and 55 and the Ju 88s from KG 54 were deployed in this operation, with KGr.100 and III/KG 26 functioning as Pathfinders; altogether about 200 aircraft. All participating crews went through hell over Moscow, for its anti-aircraft defences were comparable with those of London. Hardly had the first bombs been dropped by KGr.100 and II/KG

26 than a deadly net of anti-aircraft fire went up extending from 500 metres to an altitude of 3,000 metres. It was an absolute inferno: below explosions and fires and above inter-weaving tracer from the light anti-aircraft and bursting shells from the heavy guns. When the attack was resumed the following night only 159 aircraft were operational, and the third day only 100. Altogether, 76 attacks were made on Moscow in 1941 but, apart from the three raids mentioned above, the others were only harassing sorties involving at the most ten aircraft. Apart from that, the Luftwaffe at this point had already been weakened to such an extent that the only raids that could be flown were those against points of main effort. II/KG 26 was still operating in the Mediterranean area: on 10 September He 111H-6s of this *Gruppe* attacked military installations along the Suez canal, and Cairo itself on the night of 16/17 September.

On the Eastern Front 536 bombers had been lost by the end of September 1941 and a further 337 had returned with damage necessitating their being sent back to Germany for repair. In cold statistics, this meant that the Luftwaffe had started the war against the Soviet Union with 510 bombers, and almost double that number had been put out of action in just three months. The loss of aircraft was bad enough, but much more serious was the loss of life. Until then operational crews had mainly consisted of airmen who had been trained more or less under peacetime conditions. Now, however, training periods were continually being shortened, which meant that younger crews were flying operationally with little experience—and the losses mounted.

On 17 November 1941 the German public was shattered by the news that *Generaloberst* Ernst Udet, Chief of Aircraft Procurement, had 'crashed and been killed testing a new type of aircraft'. In actual fact he had committed suicide in despair at the wrong direction taken by the development of the Luftwaffe for which he felt himself to be, in part, responsible. Together with other dignitaries the General of Fighters was also supposed to attend the State funeral ordered by Hitler. *Oberst* Werner Mölders was, at this time, on the Eastern Front inspecting JG 77. He took off with his Adjutant, *Major* Wenzel for the long flight to Berlin in an He 111 belonging to a bomber *Gruppe* at Kherson. His pilot, *Oberleutnant* Kolbe, was an experienced 'old stager'. The aircraft landed at Lvov to refuel and continued its journey on 23 November. Germany lay under a thick layer of fog and, over Poland, a drop in oil pressure put one engine out of action. Mölders, however, ordered the pilot to fly on to Breslau-Gandau where he was certain to pick up a rail connection. As they approached to land the other engine suddenly

cut out as well. Kolbe managed to scrape the aircraft over a cable-railway, but it crashed just short of the airfield. *Oberst* Mölders was sitting in the observers seat next to the pilot and both were killed instantly.

An He 111, the communications aircraft of the C-in-C *Luftflotte* 3, *Generalfeldmarschall* Hugo Sperrle, was involved in another fatal accident. The victim of this one was the creator of the German *Autobahn* system and the organisation named after him, Dr Todt, who crashed on a flight to Munich on 8 February 1942. The circumstances of this second, fateful accident have never been completely cleared up.

The early onset of winter, which the German forces were in no way equipped to withstand, brought the German advance into the Soviet Union to a halt.

In Africa the Italians were in no position to maintain supplies to the Italo-German forces in North Africa and Rommel was forced to fall

Oberst Werner Mölders, the General of Fighters, with his ADC *Major* Wenzel (right) on 21 November 1941 shortly before his last flight

Left top: An He 111H over the Soviet landscape and *(below)* a formation of He 111Hs flying east over the clouds. The yellow band around the rear fuselage was obligatory on all Luftwaffe aircraft operating on the Eastern Front

General Kübler of the *Gebirgsjäger* as a passenger in an He 111

General Udet, in charge of aircraft procurement, and General Jeschonnek, Chief of the Luftwaffe General Staff, felt responsible for the mistakes in the Luftwaffe's long-term planning and both committed suicide

General Pflugbeil, commander of IV *Fliegerkorps,* leaving his communications He 111H to visit II/JG 77 in the southern sector of the Eastern Front. On his left *Hauptmann* von Prittwitz, on his right *Hauptmann* Dr Stormer

173

Pilot of an He 111
flying at 6,000 m
(19,600 ft) altitude
wearing his oxygen
mask, with the
fuselage nose glazing
reflecting evily in his
sunglasses

Pilot's instrument
panel and controls in
an He 111H. Like in all
He 111s, the control
column could be
swung over to the
right in an emergency

He 111P-6 of KG 4 *General Wever*. Note how quickly the bombs are forced by airstream from upwards to downwards-pointing position on leaving the vertical fuselage bomb magazine

He 111H-6 returning from a sortie on the Eastern Front. *Below:* One of the He 111 bombers of Junck's detachment abandoned in Iraq. Note the hastily overpainted Luftwaffe insignia

back on the Gazala Line. The Soviets began their winter offensive. Then came the thunderclap of Pearl Harbor. The situation for Germany and its allies had become very serious but was to deteriorate still further: 1942 was to bring the turning point, starting the downward trend.

Since a limited bombing offensive was to be maintained against Britain and since the He 111H-6 did not quite meet the demands made on it in this sector, a special night bomber was being developed in Marienehe, the He 111H-10. As this version was only to be used over Britain only a limited series was laid on. The armament of the H-10 was reduced to five MG 15s, as it was felt that there was *still* no reason to expect strong opposition from British night fighters. On the other hand, the armour protection was strengthened. To counter the increased use by the British of barrage balloons at night the He 111H-10 was equipped with the so-called *Kuto-Nase*: the leading edges of the wings were covered only by a thin skinning under which a steel cutter was located capable of severing a balloon cable in a fraction of a second should the aircraft fly into one in the dark. On account of the heavy armour only a maximum 2,000 kg (4,410 lb) of bombs could be carried. Whereas until then the night bombers had used only a make-shift camouflage of washable black paint over their standard colour scheme, the He 111H-10s were delivered from the factory with their undersurfaces, fuselage sides and fin/rudder assemblies already sprayed black. The upper surfaces of the fuselage, wings and the tailplane kept their normal black-green (RLM 70/71) segmented colour scheme.

The threatening situation in the Mediterranean caused Hitler still further to weaken the already weak Luftwaffe on the Eastern Front,

and *Generalfeldmarschall* Kesselring was ordered to transfer *Luftflotte* 2 from the central sector of the Eastern Front to airfields in Sicily and Libya—and that at the very moment when two Soviet army groups were about to attack. In the event, the whole *Luftflotte* was not transferred to the Mediterranean, but only the long-range reconnaissance aircraft of Aufkl.Gr(F) 122, JG 53, and II *Fliegerkorps* less JG 51, *Schnellkampfgruppe* 210 (SKGr.210), and the transports of KGr.zbV 102. *Generalfeldmarschall* Kesselring was appointed C-in-C South and made responsible for all German

Above and left: When *Luftflotte* 2 was switched to the south, II *Fliegerkorps* was one of the units moved to the Mediterranean. Its commanding officer, *Generaloberst* Bruno Loerzer was flown to Sicily in He 111H-6 DB + QJ piloted by *Sonderführer* (Special Duties officer) Köhler

operations in the Mediterranean area. The bombers of II *Fliegerkorps* became operational over the Mediterranean in March 1942. In the period between 23 and 26 March they completely destroyed the British Malta convoy MW 10 consisting of four ships, totalling 29,244 gross tons. At about the same time in the far north the battle began against the convoys bound for the Soviet Union and here the He 111H-6 was to show that the He 111 was far from obsolete. At the beginning of April the air offensive against Malta started in which KG 53, equipped with He 111H-6 bombers was one of the units taking part.

The night bombing raids by RAF Bomber Command were also intensifying, and the first four-engined bombers, the Halifax, Stirling and Lancaster had already made their appearance over Germany.

And across the Atlantic the American armament industry was just getting into stride: the race for aerial supremacy had begun.

When carrying a bomb load exceeding 2,500 kg (5,512 lb) the He 111 needed take off assistance which was provided by the so-called *R-Geräte* RATOG units. *Right:* The rockets are ignited immediately both engines are running at full throttle. *Centre:* The *R-Geräte* are developing full power and the aircraft speeds forward. *Bottom:* The jettisonable *R-Geräte* have done their job and the He 111 takes off at a steep angle

In 1942 a film was made at Marienehe—*Die Jüngsten der Luftwaffe* (The Youngest of the Luftwaffe)—as recruitment propaganda for the Luftwaffe ground crew preparatory schools. These two stills from that film show *(top)* changing the engine in record time and *(below)* the instructor, *Herr* Semrau explaining details to an apprentice

The Twin Heinkel He 111

The advent of the cargo glider led to further progress in the evolution of the He 111. The success of the DFS 230 glider had led to the development of the Messerschmidt Me 321 large-capacity cargo glider. Difficulties in finding suitable glider-towing aircraft had prompted General Udet, Chief of Aircraft Procurement, when visiting Heinkel to suggest a 'Siamese twin' construction of two He111 H-6s—particularly since the 'Troika' towing method using three Bf 110s was causing too many problems.

During the early months of 1941 a start was made at Marienehe on the construction of two prototype aircraft. Basically the conversion was very simple: the port wing was removed from one He 111H-6 and the starboard wing from another and a connecting centre piece on which a fifth engine was mounted and with the same aerofoil as the wing sections to be joined fitted in between. The two prototypes of this version, designated He 111Z (for *Zwilling* = Twin) were completed in the late autumn of 1941 and underwent exhaustive tests at the factory. Three months later, both aircraft could be handed over to the Rechlin Test Centre with a clear conscience. Here both He 111Zs were again put through exhaustive tests and the first towing trials were carried out, proceeding to the entire satisfaction of the Luftwaffe pilots, whereupon the RLM Supply Office (GL/E2)

placed an order for ten He 111 Z-1 glider tugs. All ten aircract were delivered from the Heinkel works already by the spring of 1942. At long last the Luftwaffe had a towing aircraft that could develop 6,700 hp at take-off and lift off the giant Me 321 without complications. Trials showed that the He 111Z, in spite of its unwieldiness around all three axes and certain heaviness on the controls, could be flown comparatively easily when making banking turns. Two glider-towing *Schlepp-Staffeln* of He 111Z tugs and Me 321 gliders were formed intended for use in the planned invasion of Malta and in the later air-landing operation at Astrakhan and Baku on the Caspian Sea. In the event none of these operations ever took place. It was not until the winter of 1942/43 that these *S-Staffeln* were transferred to the Eastern Front to take part in supplying Stalingrad, but the airfields at Pitomnik and Gumrak were overrun by Soviet forces before the towing combinations became operational. The subsequent use of the He 111Z/Me 321s is described in another chapter.

Top: The first He 111 *Zwilling* DS + EQ. *Centre:* An He 111Z-1 under camouflage netting early in 1943. *Bottom left:* The central Jumo 211F-2 engine with the enormous Me 321 glider in the background. *Bottom right:* The extraordinary combination of an He 111Z with Me 321 glider in tow ▶

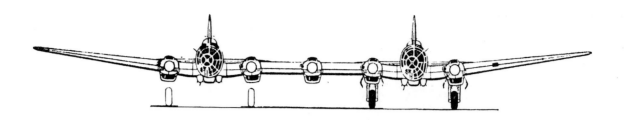

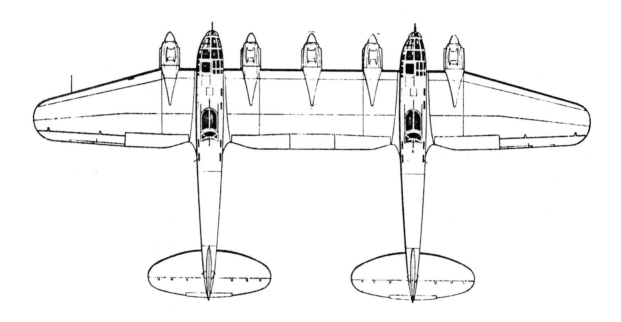

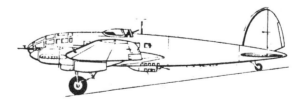

Three-view of the He 111Z-1

182

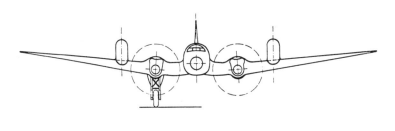

Proposal for detachable wing surface cabins for aircraft

Possible uses of aircraft with detachable wing cabins
There are several possible uses for aircraft with such detachable wing-mounted cabins:

1) For the transport of paratroops

The two wing-mounted cabins of an He 111 can accommodate 16-20 men (the Ju 52 can transport only 12).

The accommodation of paratroops in two separate cabins has the advantage that two men can jump simultaneously. This means that the troops can land in a smaller area.

If bombers are used to transport paratroops the enemy would not immediately realise the purpose of their operation. At present, if a formation of Ju 52s appears over enemy territory the enemy knows at once that they are carrying paratroops since this is the only purpose for which this type of aircraft is used over enemy territory.

2) For the transport of ground personnel

At present, a bomber unit is unable to transport its ground crews in its combat aircraft, necessitating the use of additional transport aircraft or gliders. Using detachable wing cabins, the entire ground staff could be transported together with the unit, making it extremely mobile. Once the wing cabins have been removed the aircraft immediately again become available for combat duties.

3) For the transport of wounded

Up to eight severely wounded soldiers can be transported on stretchers in the wing cabins.

4) For the transport of cargo

Petrol, bombs, ammunition, spare parts, tools, equipment, rations, etc. can be transported in these wing cabins.

(translation of an official Heinkel document)

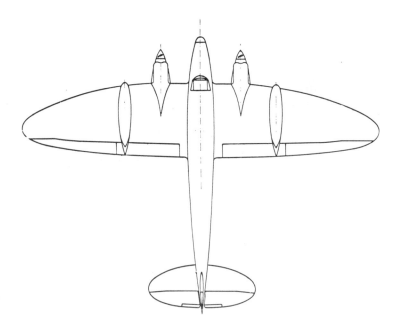

A sketch of a basic He 111 with detachable wing cabins for transporting personnel

At the end of April and beginning of May 1942 the torpedo aircraft of Kü.Fl.Gr.906 had their first successes in the battle against the Arctic convoys: they succeeded in sinking three ships totalling 15,808 gross tons from the PQ 15 to Murmansk.

I and II *Gruppen* of KG 26 with He 111H-4 torpedo-bombers were now transferred to Bardufoss and Banak in Norway to join in the fight against the Russian convoys.

However, the development of German torpedo aviation was an unhappy one, falling victim to the bitter rivalry between the Luftwaffe and the *Kriegsmarine*. The Navy knew exactly how effective attacks with aerial torpedoes were, but were allowed neither to train nor to instruct aircrews for this task. In the Luftwaffe airmen flying torpedo aircraft were basically bomber pilots and believed it to be more effective to drop bombs direct onto the target than to bring their torpedoes in low-level attack to about 1,500 m from the target and then launch them to make their own way. However, Göring himself had witnessed the successes of Italian torpedo-bombers in the Mediterranean and now wanted to have something similar as well. As a result the two *Gruppen* of KG 26 were sent to Grosseto in Italy to be retrained for torpedo attacks. The first sortie made by I/KG 26 against ships of convoy PQ 16 was abortive. But things went better on 26 May: Ju 88 A-4s from KG 30 and the He 111H-4s mounted a continuous attack and damaged a number of freighters—two of them so badly that they had to be sunk by the escorting destroyers. The next morning, seven He 111H-4s from I/KG 26 in Bardufoss attacked the convoy and torpedoed two ships, halting them. They were then sunk by Ju 88s from KG 30—but with bombs.

Also on 26 May *Generaloberst* Rommel had started a new offensive in North Africa supported by bombers of II *Fliegerkorps*, including He 111s from KG 53. Four days later the RAF bombed Cologne—their first raid on a German city with over 1,000 bombers (1,047 to be exact). Of the 868 bombers that reached the target, 40 were shot down and 40 others damaged, of which 12 crashed on landing. But 474 killed, 5,000 injured and 45,000 homeless at Cologne was a terrible toll. And that was just the beginning. On 18 June Major General Spaatz had taken over command of the US 8th Army Air Force in Britain and it was obvious that the Americans would not be long in joining the bombing as well.

In the meantime operational experience had shown that the He 111H-10 needed further improvement and this led to the He 111H-11. On this version, armament and armour were strengthened, the dorsal gun position was given better protection and was now completely enclosed, and the 7.9 mm MG 15 was replaced by a 13 mm MG 131; the nose gun position carried a 20 mm MG/FF cannon, and the ventral gun position had its single MG 15 replaced by a twin-barrel MG 81Z. The MG 15s were retained only in the beam positions. The He 111H-11 carried five SC 250 bombs on external racks under the fuselage and another 1,000 kg of bombs, mostly incendiaries, in the fuselage. Later the 7.9 mm MG 15s in the beam positions were replaced by twin-barrel MG 81Zs (*Rüstsatz* 1), changing the designation to He 111H-11/R1. Subsequently, these machines were fitted with glider-towing equipment in the fuselage tail, redesignated as He 111H-11/R2, and used to tow Go 242 cargo gliders.

The British, meanwhile, were suffering a number of reverses in the far north. On 5 July 1942, convoy PQ 13 which had left Murmansk on 27 June for the return journey to England ran into a minefield that the British had laid themselves and lost five ships sunk. This was closely followed by an even greater tragedy. On 27 June a FW 200C of I/KG 40 spotted the large convoy PQ 17, but then lost contact in fog. However, two U-boats found the convoy again off Jan Mayen Island. On 2 July PQ 17 was attacked by torpedo-carrying He 115 floatplanes of Kü.Fl.Gr.406, but without success. On 3 July came Ju 88s of KG 30 with bombs, but still without success. Then one ship was torpedoed and sunk by a U-boat, and that seemed to break the spell. At 13.15 hrs 25 He 111H-4s of KG 26 attacked with torpedoes hitting and stopping four ships.

At 18.20 hrs the 25 He 111H-4s attacked again with torpedoes, this time hitting three ships. Then the U-boats and Ju 88s took over. The result of this action was 24 ships sunk totalling 143,997 gross tons. Not much was left of convoy PQ 17, but this success was never to be repeated.

The torpedo aircraft had their turn again with the next supply convoy for the Soviet Union, this time, however, with severe losses to themselves. Stalin had been bombarding the Western Allies with demands for further deliveries of war materials, terming the quantities delivered to date as derisory. To placate the Soviets convoy PQ 18 was assembled in Loch Ewe in Scotland and started its journey on 1 September 1942. Protection consisted of the escort carrier *Avenger* (11,420 tons) with 15 aircraft, the light cruiser *Scylla* (5,450 tons), 16 destroyers, two submarines and a whole host of trawlers, corvettes and smaller warships. On 18 September the convoy was spotted off Jan Mayen Island by a BV 138 flying boat from Kü.Fl.Gr.706. The long-distance reconnaissance *Staffeln* at Banak, Kirkenes and Bardufoss immediately despatched Ju 88D-1s to keep contact. The aircraft relieved each other

at the end of their maximum flight endurance without a hitch. It was not until 12 September that the British discovered they were being shadowed by the Germans. Several Hurricanes took off at once from *Avenger* but the Ju 88 had already disappeared. The first attack on the convoy came from below, not, as the British had expected, from above. On the morning of 13 September a submarine fired a quadruple salvo claiming two of the transports. The escorting destroyers tried without success to sink the U-boat with depth charges. The battle had been joined. In the afternoon of the same day a dozen Ju 88A-4s from KG 30 appeared, as a diversion from the main attack as it turned out, but their high-level attack missed the target. Then I *Gruppe* of KG 26 made its appearance under *Major* Klümper who had been in charge of the torpedo training in Grosseto. The 24 He 111H-4 torpedo-bombers came from Bardufoss and should have been led onto the target by the shadowing aircraft. But the radio contact did not work properly and Klümper's formation had to make a wide sweep before it could find the convoy. The aircraft were flying only a few metres above the waves to keep below the radar beams of the British warships. Klümper now divided his formation into two groups of 12 aircraft each. Following on behind them came III/KG 26 under *Hauptmann* Klaus Nocken. Altogether at this moment about 40 He 111H-6s were heading towards the convoy. The ships' anti-aircraft guns put up a dense curtain of fire in front of the approaching He 111s. Klümper's first objective was to put the aircraft carrier out of action, but this was nowhere to be seen having steamed after the Ju 88s. The He 111s then climbed to about 40 metres above the sea and attacked the freighters. Some torpedo-bombers damaged by the heavy British anti-

Left top: He 111H-10 of 1.*Staffel*/KG 76. This version featured the so-called *'Kuto-Nase'* wing leading edge balloon cable cutters. *Centre:* Soviet photograph of a shot down He 111H-10. *Bottom:* He 111H-11 of 1./KG 76. This version introduced an 13 mm MG 131 in the fully enclosed dorsal position

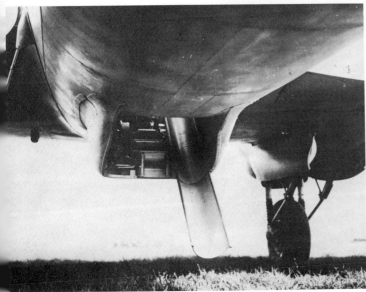

Top: An He 111H-11 dropping paratroops. *Centre left:* Target towing equipment on an He 111H-11. *Right:* The beam MG 15 position on the He 111H-11. *Bottom:* He 111H-11

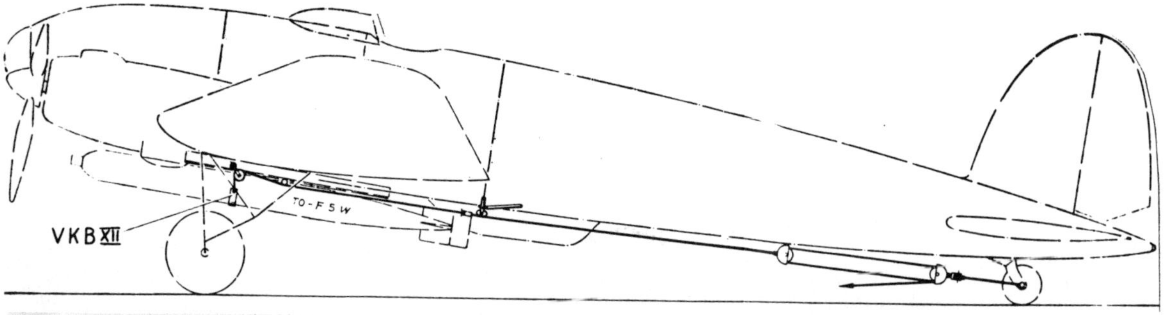
VKB XII
TO-F5W

▲ *Above and below:* FZ 2000 torpedo hoisting equipment with block-and-tackle fitted on the
▼ He 111H-12

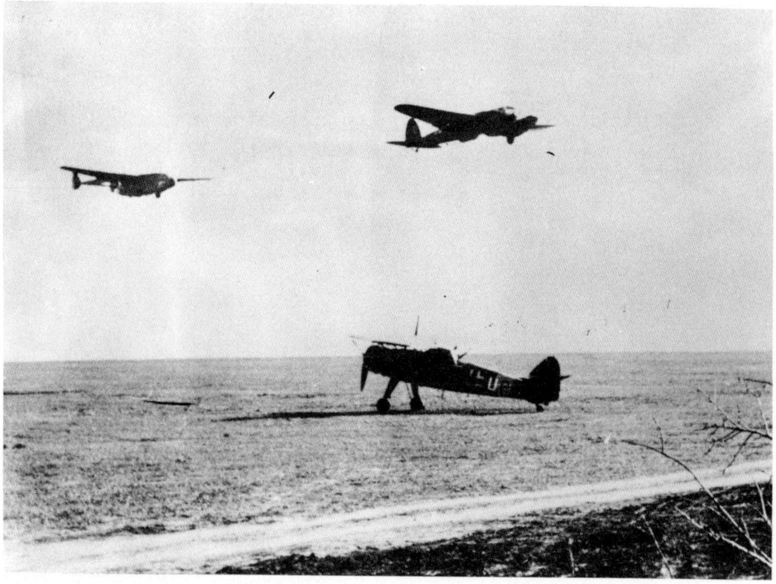

◀ *Left and opposite page:* He 111H-11 as towing aircraft for the Go 242 cargo gliders. The two top pictures show take-offs with rocket assistance. The Hs 126 short-range reconnaissance aircraft (in the foreground) were used to tow the smaller DFS 230 glider

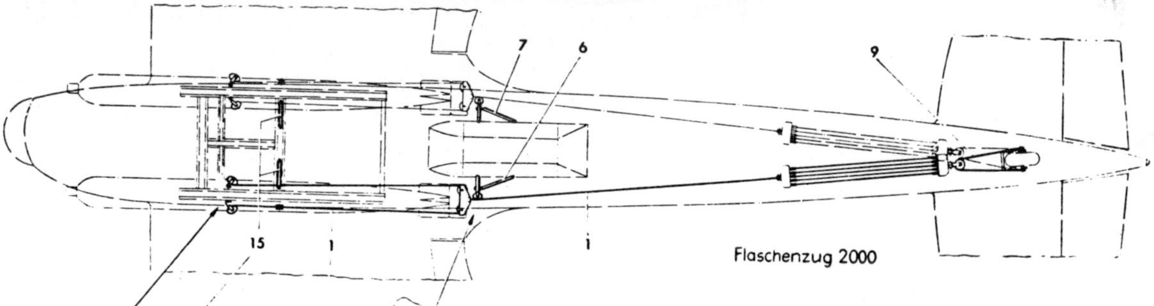
7
6
9
15
1
1
Flaschenzug 2000

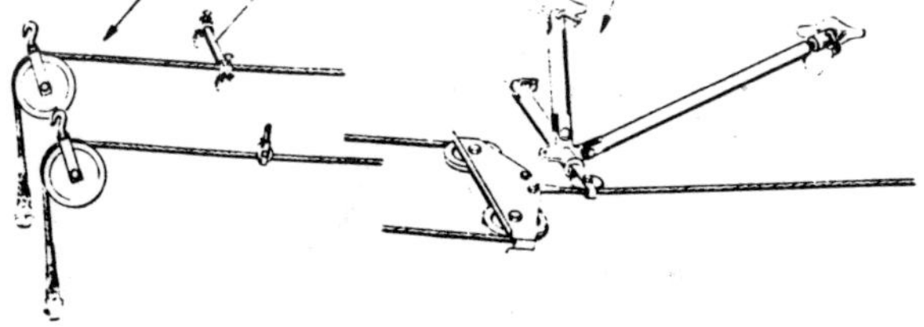

Pos.	Anzahl	Benennung	Teil-Nr.
1	1	Heißseilzug für LT	111.9137-29
6	1	Bock für Heißvorrichtung, links	111.9122-110
7	1	Bock für Heißvorrichtung, rechts	111.9122-111
9	1	Abspanndrahtseil	111.9122-113
15	2	Umlenkvorrichtung	111.9122-132

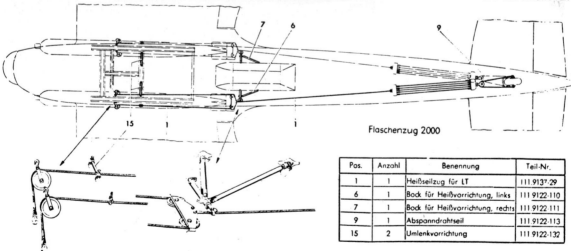

These four pictures of an He 111H-6 of KG 26 stationed at Stavanger-Sola in summer 1941 give a particularly clear view of the torpedoes and their attachment. The LT F5b, a German development of original Norwegian and Italian designs, was 5·36 m (17 ft 7 in) long, weighed 765 kg (1,686·5 lb) and had an explosive charge of 185 kg (408 lb). Its maximum running range was 2,000 m (2,190 yds)

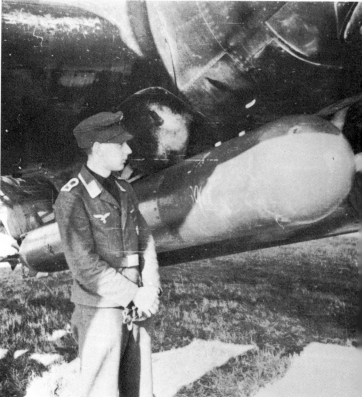

The He 111H12 was a specially modified missile launching version, differing externally by having no ventral gondola. These three pictures show trials with the BV 143 rocket-powered surface torpedo glider near Zinnowitz on the Baltic coast. The BV 143 was originally intended to carry a modified 500 kg (1,102 lb) armour-piercing bomb launched about 5,000-6,000 m (5,470-6,560 yds) from the target. Its Walter liquid-fuel rocket motor developed a thrust of 600 kg (1,323 lb) for 60 secs. At least three different versions of the BV 143 were evolved, but the various control and technical problems could not be overcome

The Blohm & Voss L 10 *Friedensengel* (Angel of Peace) torpedo glider was also test-launched from the He 111H-12. This auxiliary lift and stabilizing attachment was intended to increase the glide distance of air-launched torpedoes, but the trials could not be successfully concluded before the end of hostilities

The Hs 293 was a radio-controlled rocket-boosted bomb intended for use against shipping targets. Development began early in 1940, and the basic design was evolved in many variants. Most launching trials were carried out from specially equipped He 111Hs. *Above:* The Hs 293D television-guided version. At least 70 were produced for trials. *Below:* The Hs 293A was guided by the bomb aimer via a single control lever activating the FuG 203b *Kehl III* transmitter installed in the dorsal gun position which sent control impulses to the FuG 230 *Strassburg* receiver fitted in the tail of the missile. These guided bombs were used on several successful operations launched from Do 217 and He 177 carriers

aircraft fire were forced to release their torpedoes prematurely but the rest approached to about 1,000 metres from the ships. More than 20 torpedoes splashed into the water and sought their targets. Then all hell was let loose. Columns of water, explosions and spreading conflagrations made it impossible to gauge the results, but within a few moments eight ships had sunk. The British were so shaken by this attack that the first accounts reported the raid had been carried out by 100 He 111s and that 15 had been shot down. In actual fact, only five He 111s had been lost.

The next day I/KG 26 attacked again but only 22 aircraft were operational. This time, however, the fighters from *Avenger* were at hand and the He 111s were unsuccessful, five being shot down and a further nine so damaged as to be temporarily out of action. The He 111 torpedo-bombers attacked again on 19 and 20 September, but managed to sink only one more ship, while the Ju 88s of KG 30 had absolutely no success to report. In all, the two *Gruppen* of KG 26 had lost 20 crews, that is half their establishment. Of the 37 ships in the convoy 27 reached their destination with enough equipment for a dozen divisions.

In North Africa things at first went smoothly as far as the El Alamein narrows, but that was the end: Rommel's forces had hardly 50 tanks left and a further attempt to break through to Egypt failed.

The situation in the air on the Western front deteriorated daily as RAF Bomber Command's formations stepped up their attacks on Germany. On the German side almost all they were able to do was to mount harrassing raids by fighter-bombers from JG 2 and JG 26. On 23 October the British 8th Army under Lt. General Montgomery began its offensive at El Alamein which broke through the Italo-German front.

On 7 and 8 November Allied troops under General Eisenhower landed in Tunisia and Algeria. On 19 November the Soviet offensive at Stalingrad began, leading to the bottling up of the German 6th Army under *Generaloberst* Paulus.

Meanwhile, at Heinkel's further efforts had been made to improve the performance of the He 111, and new uses were continually being sought for this reliable aircraft since the new He 177 bomber was experiencing such difficulties with its engines that there was no question of its regular operational employment, but the tragedy of the He 177 is another story. The catastrophic results of the 1940 ban on development work were now being felt. The new designs, whose prototypes were flying in 1940/41 should by now have been being produced in large series but none of them had yet reached that stage. At the end of 1941 *Generalfeldmarschall* Erhard Milch had declared that 'Russia had been crushed and there was no more need for new developments'. To be sure, the numbers of machines being produced by the German aircraft industry continued to rise, but they were all old pre-1939 types and a continuous process of tinkering about with them was going on in order to improve performance.

At the beginning of 1940 the RLM had invited tenders for a new weapon. Among other requirements was one for 'the creation of a bomb for use against merchant and lightly armoured ships which would reduce to a minimum the danger to attacking aircraft from enemy anti-aircraft fire'.

The result of this requirement was the development of guided missiles and flying bombs by Dr Richard Vogt of Blohm & Voss and Prof Herbert Wagner of Henschel Aircraft Works. These novel bombs were to be carried by the He 111 and Ju 88, although trials of these guided weapons (BV 143, 246, 268 and Hs 293, 294, 295, 296 and 298) were carried out exclusively with He 111s. In this context the He 111H-12 was intended for the Henschel flying bombs and the He 111H-15 for the Blohm & Voss missiles. In both cases the ventral gondola was removed in order to make room for the wings of the flying bombs. Trials of the Hs 293 took place at the Luftwaffe Test Establishment E-4 at Peenemünde. The missile was guided by a radio via FuG 203b *Kehl III* in the aircraft: the Hs 293 carried the FuG 230b *Strassburg* which received and passed on the control impulses. These tests took quite some time and the first operational sorties were not flown until 1943. The He 111H-12 had a four-man crew and a defensive armament of five MG 15s. The He 111H-15 was designed to carry a maximum of three BV 246 missiles. As it proved impossible during the trials to overcome the guidance problems successfully the He 111H-15 (only a few were completed) were re-converted to ordinary He 111H-10 night bombers.

In the autumn of 1942 large-scale production began at Marienehe and Oranienburg of the new He 111H-16 series. This version was largely similar to the H-11 except that the bomb-load could be varied by the use of different *Rüstsätze* (Standard Equipment sets), maximum load being 3,250 kg (7,165 lb). This overload, however, necessitated the use of the so-called *R-Geräte* (jettisonable rockets) to assist take-off, added to which the He 111H-16 then only had a range of 740 km (460 miles). With a normal bomb-load of 1,000 kg (2,205 lb) the range was 2,700 to 2,900 km (1,678 to 1,802 miles). As usual, range = outward flight at maximum continuous power to the point of bombing, return flight at cruising power, both at 5,000 m (16,405 ft). The armament of the He 111H-16 was very heavy: a 20 mm MG/FF cannon in the nose position, one MG 131 in the dorsal position, one twin-barrel MG 81Z in the ventral position, and two twin-barrel MG 81Z machine guns in beam positions.

The He 111H-14 was a 'pathfinder' variant of the H-16 carrying a complement of six on account of the augmented radio equipment; only 30 of these machines were built. Another 20 were completed as He 111H-14/R2 towing aircraft for the Go 242 cargo gliders. As early as the spring of 1942 the He 111H-6 were used as transport aircraft to supply the Kholm outpost where a mixed combat group of some 3,500 men formed from remnants of various decimated formations and led by *Generalmajor* Scherer, commander of 281 Inf. Div., were surrounded by strong Soviet forces. When the losses of Ju 52s from KGr.zbV 172 landing at Kholm reached intolerable levels KG 4 '*General Wever*' was detailed to supply the cut-off troops. As the quantities that could be dropped into the pocket at Kholm in containers proved to be inadequate, a policy was adopted of using cargo gliders as 'disposable equipment', towing them at low altitude and with fixed rudders as close as possible to the target and then releasing them to land into the German lines. These measures enabled Scherer's force to hold out until early May 1943 when they were relieved by 411 Inf.Rgt. which managed to break through the Soviet front.

The supply operation for the Demyansk pocket was carried out at the same time as that of Kholm.

Here II Army Corps under General von Brockdorf-Ahlefeld and elements of X Army Corps were surrounded by six Soviet armies. Once again the He 111H-6s of KG 4 took over the supply operations until the arrival of the hastily collected *Kampfgeschwader z.b.V.*

Top: The He 111H-15 was intended as carrier for three glider bombs to be launched at night from high altitude. Due to inconclusive results of launching tests the few He 111H-15s built were completed as ordinary night bombers and used on the Eastern Front
Centre: He 111H-6 with three Blohm & Voss BV 246 *Hagelkorn* (Hailstone) guided glider bombs
Bottom left: BV 246 glider bombs with different warheads. Originally designated BV 226, this air-launched missile was proposed as a FZG 76 (V-1) replacement but rejected because of poor target accuracy. Resurrected in 1943, the BV 246 was evolved in several versions, mainly with very high aspect ratio concrete wings. Although tests were promising and more than 600 BV 246B, E and F missiles were available, the operational trials were never satisfactorily concluded

Above: Only 30 He 111H-14s were completed. Fitted with special radio equipment including FuG *Samos* and FuG 351 *Korfu* these machines were intended as 'pathfinders' for night bombers and chiefly used by *Kampfgruppe* 100. *Below:* This He 111H-14 *Werk Nr.* 5101 was so badly shot up by RAF night fighters that it had to make a belly landing on return. Note the KGr.100 insignia

Two more photographs of crash-landed He 111H-14 *Werk Nr.*5101. Some of the combat damage is clearly seen

The He 111H-16 was the last version of the He 111 to be produced in large numbers and could be used for a variety of tasks by fitting different *Rüstsätze* (standard equipment sets). The lower picture shows trials with flexible hot air pipes to warm up the engines before starting in very cold weather conditons

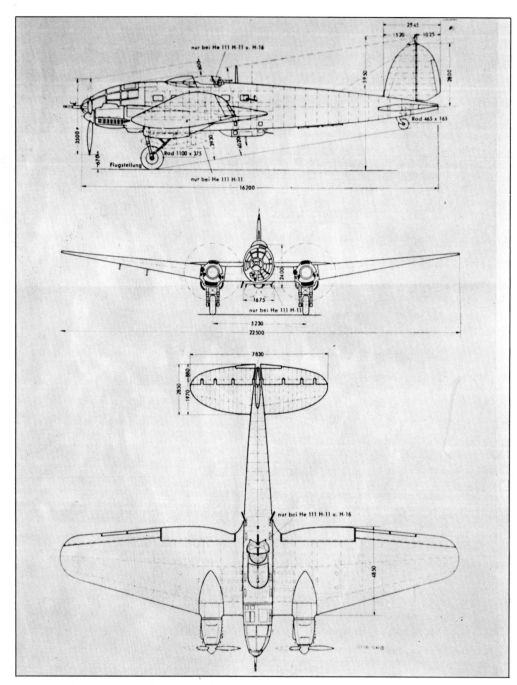

Factory drawings of the He 111H-11 and H-16

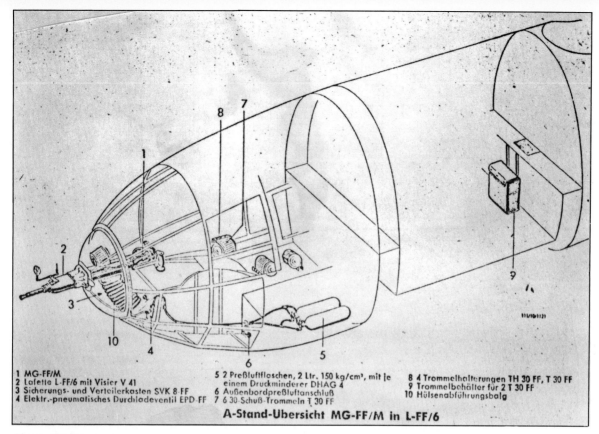

1 MG-FF/M
2 Lafette L-FF/6 mit Visier V 41
3 Sicherungs- und Verteilerkasten SVK 8-FF
4 Elektr.-pneumatisches Durchladeventil EPD-FF

5 2 Preßluftflaschen, 2 Ltr. 150 kg/cm³, mit je einem Druckminderer DHAG 4
6 Außenbordpreßluftanschluß
7 6 30-Schuß-Trommeln T 30 FF

8 4 Trommelhalterungen TH 30 FF, T 30 FF
9 Trommelbehälter für 2 T 30 FF
10 Hülsenabführungsbalg

A-Stand-Ubersicht MG-FF/M in L-FF/6

Above: Flexible nose gun installation: MG-FF/M in L-FF/6 mount
1. 20 mm MG-FF/M cannon
2. L-FF/6 mount with V 41 sight
3. SVK 8-FF fuse and distributor box
4. EPD-FF electro-pneumatic cocking valve
5 Two compressed air bottles, 2 ltr capacity 150 kg/cm² (2,133 lb/in²) each, with DHAG 4 pressure reducing unit
6. External compressed air connection .
7. Six 30-round T 30-FF ammunition drums
8. 4 TH 30-FF and T 30-FF drum mountings
9. Container for two T 30-FF drums
10. Empty cartridge disposal case

He 111H-16 defensive armament and arcs of fire
1. 20 mm MG-FF/M cannon
2. 13 mm MG 131
3. 7·9 mm MG 81 (one in each beam position)
4. 7·9 mm twin-barrel MG 81Z

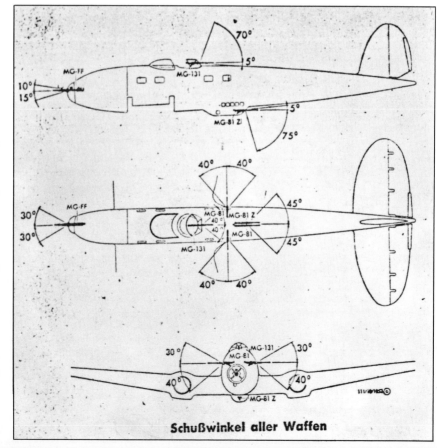

Schußwinkel aller Waffen

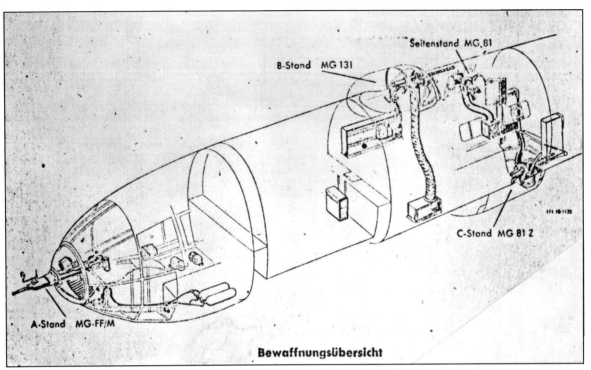

Seitenstand MG 81

B-Stand MG 131

C-Stand MG 81 Z

A-Stand MG-FF/M

Bewaffnungsübersicht

Above: General view of defensive armament

Left: View of dorsal position: WL 131 AL with MG 131 B2

1. 13 mm MG 131 B2
2. Sight
3. WL 131 AL roller mount
4. 131 ammunition belt
5. Container for full ammunition belts
6. Belt feed
7. Diverter for empty ammunition belts
8. Empty ammunition belt and cartridge diverter pipe
9. Container for empty ammunition belts
10. Stop to prevent hitting own tail

1 MG 131 B 2
2 Visier
3 Walzenlafette WL 131 AL
4 Gurt 131
5 Vollgurtbehälter
6 Gurtzuführung
7 Leergurtableitung
8 Leergurt- und Hülsenableitung
9 Leergutbehälter
10 Waffenabweiser

Übersicht B-Stand WL 131 AL mit MG 131 B2

202

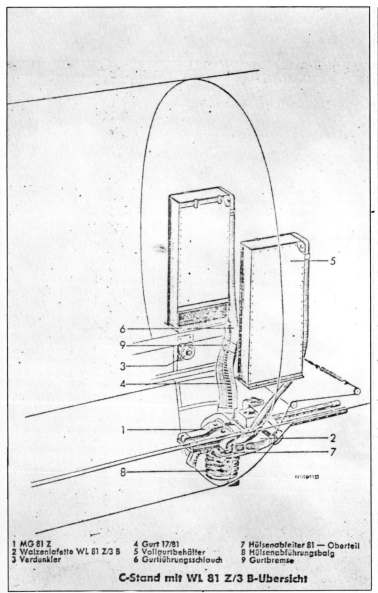

C-Stand mit WL 81 Z/3 B-Übersicht

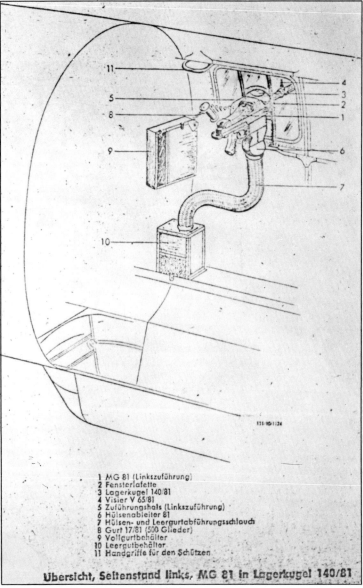

Übersicht, Seitenstand links, MG 81 in Lagerkugel 140/81

Ventral gun position with WL 81 Z/3B

1. 7·9 mm MG 81Z twin-barrel machine gun
2. WL 81 Z/3B roller mount
3. Dimming switch
4. 17/81 ammunition belt
5. Container for full ammunition belts
6. Ammunition belt feed hose
7. 81 empty cartridge diverter, top section
8. Empty cartridge diverter pipe
9. Belt brake

Beam (port) gun position: MG 81 in 140/81 ball mount

1. 7·9 mm MG 81 (left-hand feed)
2. Window mounting
3. 140/81 ball mount
4. V 65/81 sight
5. Feed collar (left-hand feed)
6. 81 empty cartridge diverter
7. Diverter pipe for empty cartridges and belts
8. 17/81 ammunition belt (500 rds)
9 Container for full ammunition belts
10. Container for empty ammunition belts
11. Hand grip for machine gunner

203

Several bomber units were impressed in the transport role for the air supply of Stalingrad. *Above:* He 111s of I/KG 100 at Dniepropetrovsk before take-off. *Below:* An He 111H-16 being waved in. Note the additional flexible MG 15 starboard side of the nose section

Above: Major Bätcher, commanding I/KG 100 during the Stalingrad supply operations. *Below:* The radio operator at work during one of these air supply flights

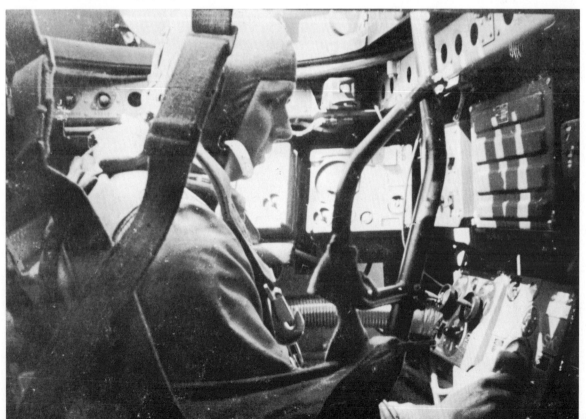

Top left: A formation of He 111H-16s on the way to Stalingrad. *Far left:* I/KG 100 on a supply flight. The attrition rate on these hazardous supply flights resulted in I/KG 100 *Staffeln* shrinking to only a fraction of their establishment.

Above and left: In addition to its supply tasks I/KG 100 also had to carry out offensive operations. Here an aircraft being loaded with SC 250 bombs assisted by Soviet POWs.

Above: Major Walter Nowotny, the famous fighter ace, on a visit in an He 111. Unfortunately reflection from the cockpit glazing makes it difficult to distinguish details

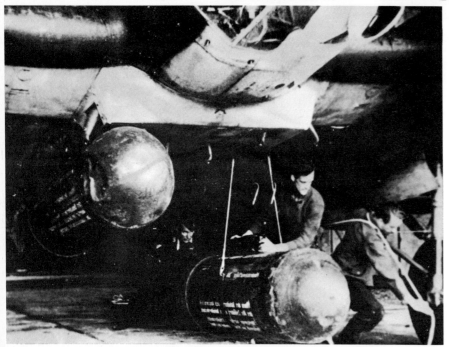

Left and above: When it was no longer possible to land in the Stalingrad 'pocket', all supplies had to be dropped in containers, with and without parachutes

(Bomber Groups for Special Purposes), as the transport *Geschwader* were still called at that time, and then the Ju 52s took over supplying the units. Demyansk was successfully held until land communications could be established with other German formations that had been forced further back. But these two successful air supply operations were to have tragic and unforseen consequences.

On 22 November 1942 the ring round the 6th Army in Stalingrad was closed at Kalatch by three Soviet army groups, the 'South-west Front' under Lt. General Vatutin, the 'Don Front' under Lt. General Rokossovsky and the 'Stalingrad Front' armies under Colonel General Yeremenko. VIII Fliegerkorps under *Generalleutnant* Martin Fiebig had seen the threatening danger and warned the Staff of the 6th Army. But Paulus' plan was to take up an all-round defensive position, a 'hedgehog', and, with the success of the air-supply of Demyansk in mind, to allow himself to be supplied from the air. Fiebig was horrified and informed *Generaloberst* von Richthofen, commanding the *Luftflotte*. It turned out that shortage of fuel had made it no longer possible for the 6th Army to break out of the encirclement and, in addition to this, a direct order had been received from Hitler that in no circumstances was the 6th Army to retire. Hitler also put pressure on Göring: the Luftwaffe must supply the 6th Army from the air. The tragedy of Stalingrad had started.

The order for the air-supply of Stalingrad reached *Luftflotte* 4 (Richthofen) on 24 November when it became apparent that, although on paper *Oberst* Förster commanding the transport services had 320 Ju 52s and Ju 86s at his disposal, only 55% of these were operational. Whereupon the *Kommodore* of KG 55 in Morozovskaya, *Oberst* Kühl, was ordered by von Richthofen to impress all He 111 units at present under his command for supplying the encircled army. At the same time he was appointed commander of *Gefechtsverband Stalingrad* (Stalingrad Combat Formation) and required to assist ground forces to repel Soviet attacks in order to prevent Tazinskaya and Morozovskaya, the jump-off bases for the supply operation, from falling into Soviet hands. *Oberst* Kühl had the following He 111 units at his disposal for this task:

Stab, I and II	
(alternating with III *Gruppe*)	
of KG 55	He 111H-6, H-16
I/KG 100	He 111H-6, H-11, H-16
I, II and III/KG 27	He 111H-6, H-16
KGr.zbV 5	He 111P and H
KGr.zbV 20	He 111D, F, P, H

From this collection of types it is evident that both KGr.zbV formations had been hastily assembled with old aircraft from the training schools that were no longer considered fit for operational service. KG 55 was commanded by *Oberst* Kühl, KG 27 by *Oberstleutnant* von Beust and I *Gruppe* of KG 100 by *Major* Bätcher. Somewhat later they were reinforced by three *Staffeln* under *Hauptleute* (Captains) Gaede, Glocke and Gratl, also equipped with older He 111 versions. KG 27 was stationed at Millerovo whilst all other He 111 units were based at Morozovskaya South and West. To secure his jumping-off bases *Oberst* Kühl was also allotted JG 3 'Udet' and a *Gruppe* each of Ju 87D dive bombers and Hs 129 close support aircraft. There was only one airfield available in the Stalingrad pocket, that at Pitomnik.

On 24 December 1942 Tazinskaya had to be evacuated and Morozovskaya the following week: operations had to be transferred to

Novocherkask and Stalino, increasing the distance to Pitomnik with a corresponding reduction in the load that could be carried. In spite of this, the He 111 units accomplished an enormous transport task under the most arduous weather and flying conditions right up to the end of the battle on 2 February 1943, flying a total of 2,566 sorties, 2,260 of them bringing supplies to the pocket. These amounted to 2,407.8 tons of food, ammunition and weapons with, in addition, 3,294.8 tons of fuel. Until 16 January 1943 each He 111 carried an average payload of 1,845 kg (4,068 lb); after that date it was reduced to only 616 kg (1,268 lb) for each air-drop. The He 111s also flew out 9,208 wounded soldiers and carried 533 sacks of mail.

During the winter months of 1942/43 the He 111 also had to undertake night fighter operations on the Eastern front, a task for which it had not been designed. Special *Nachtjagd schwärme* (night fighter sections) were formed equipped with He 111s carrying a fixed-forward armament of four 20 mm MG/FF cannon and additionally two WB 81Z weapon containers each with a twin-barrel MG 81Z machine-gun. These make-shift night fighters were used to combat Soviet aircraft supplying their partisans behind the German lines. Modified He 111s were also used to intercept the Soviet Po-2s which frequently dropped light bombs and concentrated explosive charges onto German positions at night. These biplanes were often piloted by women.

On 22 February 1943 an offensive was launched against the 'Soviet 'Voronezh Front' and 'Southwest Front' army groups by *Generalfeldmarschall* von Manstein, C-in-C of the *Heeresgruppe Süd* (Army Group South) supported by *Luftflotte* 4 under *Generalfeldmarschall* von Richthofen. In this operation the He 111 units that had functioned as supply aircraft at Stalingrad were again used in their proper bomber role, supporting 1 and 4 Panzer Armies in their successful drive eastwards. The He 111s engaged in this task often had tough exchanges with Soviet fighters, particularly with the new Lavotchkin La-5, called by the Soviets 'the wooden saviour of Stalingrad'.

The He 111Z/Me 321 towing teams which could not be used at Stalingrad then did yeoman service supplying and later evacuating the Kuban bridgehead, after which they were sent back to Germany for refurbishing. Other He 111s were also used as cargo glider tugs in the evacuation of the Kuban bridgehead.

On 15 April 1943 Hitler issued the order to prepare for the last German offensive on the Eastern front, Operation *Zitadelle*. In the meantime German transport aircraft were continuing to fly their senseless sacrificial sorties between Sicily and North Africa supplying the German forces in Tunisia. It was a very costly undertaking: dozens of the Ju 52s and all the Messerschmitt Me 323 large capacity transports engaged in this sector were shot down by British and American fighters.

The war in North Africa came to an end on 13 May 1943 when the German and Italian troops capitulated and 130,000 German and 120,000 Italian soldiers became prisoners of war. By this time only fighter-bombers were available for attacks on Britain, and at best only isolated raids were carried out by Do 217 and Ju 88 bombers.

In the period 3 to 5 June the German Luftwaffe were once more regrouping for an attack

Although by 1943 the He 111H-16 was already basically an obsolete design stretched to its limit it continued to carry out its operational tasks as a bomber, supply aircraft and glider tug ▶

in the East. Their target was the 'Molotov' tank factory in Gor'ky-Avtozavod which was within the range of German bombers. I/KG 100 under *Major* Bätcher again acted as pathfinders. Units of *Luftflotte* 4 taking part in the operation were KG 3, 27, 55 and III/KG 4, with III/KG 1, II/KG 4 and II/KG 51 from 1. *Fliegerdivision.* According to the establishment lists of these units 240 aircraft should have participated but in actual fact it was only 168, which shows how weak the German bomber *Geschwader* and *Gruppen* had become. Of this meagre total 149 aircraft reached the target and dropped 224,000 kg (493,820 lb) HE and incendiary bombs onto the tank factory. Five aircraft did not return from the raid. Only 128 bombers were operational for the second attack and dropped another 179,000 kg (394,620 lb) of bombs onto Gor'ky, this time with loss of two aircraft shot down. On the third day ground crews managed to get 154 bombers airborne and 242,000 kg (533,510 lb) of bombs were dropped on the same target. On the following day only a harrassing raid was mounted with He 111 H-16s dropping 39,000 kg (85,980 lb) of bombs. The following night another 132 German bombers, mostly He 111s, attacked the rubber plant complex in Yaroslavl. And with that the combat strength of the German bomber units was exhausted. If one compares the weight of bombs dropped by the British and the Germans it becomes painfully clear how obsolete the aircraft equipment of the German Luftwaffe had become. Thus, on the night of 20/21 June 1943 88 German bombers dropped 134,000 kg (295,420 lb) bombs on Yaroslavl whereas on 16/17 June 179 British bombers had dropped 656,000 kg (1,446,220 lb) on Cologne. In other words, double the number of bombers had dropped four times the weight of bombs.

5 July 1943 saw the beginning of Operation *Zitadelle*, the offensive against the Kursk salient. On the German side 2,000 tanks and SP assault guns and about 1,800 aircraft had been assembled. The aircraft of *Luftflotte* 6 of *Heeresgruppe Mitte* (Army Group Centre) were commanded by *Generaloberst Ritter* von Greim, II/KG 4 being the only one of his units still equipped with He 111H-16 bombers; *Luftflotte* 4, now under command of *Generaloberst* Desloch had a greater number of He 111 units: I/KG 100, III/KG 4, KG 27 and KG 55. But *Zitadelle* was born under an unlucky star. A spy ring was active within the German High Command headed by a man code-named 'Lucie' by the Soviets. He was a former Reichswehr officer called Rössler operating from Switzerland, and his reports often reached Moscow earlier than they did the High Command to whom they were addressed. Another factor leading to the failure of the offensive was the premature employment of PzKw V, the Panther tank which was not yet ready for operational use. Thus, thanks to espionage and their own long-range reconnaissance the Soviet command knew exactly what to expect and was in a position to halt the German attack. A mere four weeks later, the Soviets were able to mount a powerful counter-offensive that made deep inroads into the German lines.

Meanwhile, in the Mediterranean blow followed blow: the Allies landed in Sicily on 10 July, Mussolini was overthrown on 25 July and the Italians not only signed a truce with the Allies but entered the war against Germany.

Worst, however, was the week between 24 and 30 July: the Allied Operation 'Gomorrah', the combined attack on Hamburg by the RAF by night and US 8th Army Air Force by day. Result: shipping totalling 180,000 gross tons

Above: An He 111H-15 as a flying test bed for the Heinkel HeS 011 turbo-jet unit. *Below:* In the last months of the war He 111s were often grounded for lack of fuel. Note the special covers over gun positions.

As mentioned in the text, the He 111 was also flown as a night fighter on the Eastern Front. These pictures show an He 111H-18 used for experiments with the FuG 200 *Hohentwiel* radar at Rechlin

Above: A close-up of an He 111H-18 with the FuG 200 radar aerial array at Rechlin. *Below:* He 111H-18 with the *Zaunkönig* (Wren) device, one of the last German air interception radar developments before the end of World War II.

Above: He 111H-20 used to train FuG 220 SN-2 *Lichtenstein* radar operators at Werneuchen in 1944.
Below: An He 111H-18 radar trainer taxiing to its revetment after landing

was sunk in the port, 30,482 people were killed and 227,330 houses, 580 factories, 2,632 businesses, 24 hospitals, 277 schools—but only 80 armed forces' installations—destroyed. German night fighter airborne interception equipment and ground radar were jammed by 'Window' (strips of tin-foil), and their successes were minimal. It is only when one compares these statistics with those of German raids on Britain, particularly on Coventry and London, that the feebleness of the German Luftwaffe, even as early as 1940, can really be appreciated, and since that time it had been progressively weakened.

After the Allied landings in Sicily plans had been made to use the He 111Z/Me 321 towing teams to transport 1 and 2 Paratroop Divisions to Sicily. These two special *Staffeln* were stationed at Dijon and Istres, but the plan had to be abandoned since the distance from Istres to Sicily exceeded the range of the tug/glider combinations and, in addition, there was no airfield in Sicily large enough to accommodate the Me 321. Combinations were then made up of one He 111Z tug and two Go 242 gliders and proved very successful. In this way 1. *Fallschirmdivision* (1 Paratroop Division) was transported to southern Italy and 2 Paratroop Division to the Rome area. Experience gained with this method led to the Me 321 being dropped and to the exclusive use of the Go 242 in double, and, later on, even in triple tows.

By that time Operation *Zitadelle* had been abandoned on account of the Soviet counter-offensive on the Orel Front.

Since no replacement for the He 111H-16 had been developed, the situation on the Eastern front made it necessary for the aircraft to undergo further modifications. A revolving turret with an MG 131 at last replaced the dorsal gun position. This version with its DL 131 (DL=*Drehturmlafette* or swivel-turret mounting) went into series production as He 111H-16/R1. A further short series was built equipped for rigid bar towing of cargo gliders and designated He 111H-16/R2. Between 1938 and 1943 the DFS (German Research Establishment for Gliding Flight) had developed eleven different towing systems. The initial tow attachment version proved to be too heavy and the equipment was then further developed and improved by Weserflugzeugbau (Weser Aircraft Works). Trials of this were so successful that the version built by Weserflug went into series production and was fitted as *Rüstsatz* (Standard Equipment set) not only on the He 111 but on other aircraft as well. Depending on the task, the cargo gliders used were mainly the DFS 230 or Go 242. When carrying overloads the gliders were fitted with the so-called *R-Geräte* (jettisonable rockets) for assisted take-off.

When used as 'pathfinders', as during the raids on Gor'ky and Yaroslavl the He 111H-16 were equipped with the *Rüstsatz* 3. These He 111H-16/R3 machines did not carry external loads but were provided with additional armour protection for the crew and more extensive radio guidance equipment. There were two variants, the He 111H-16/R3/U1 and R3/U2, depending on the type of bomb-racks fitted. Some He 111H-16/R2s were used in August 1943 for Operation *Lehrgang* ('Course of Instruction'), the evacuation of Sicily.

On 18 August 1943 *Generaloberst* Jeschonnek, Chief of the Luftwaffe Staff committed suicide. Just like before him Udet, Jeschonnek had realised that he had, in part, been responsible for the mistaken direction taken in planning the development of the Luftwaffe and could see no other way out.

On 25 August 1943 the Hs 293 flying bombs

▲ *Above and below:* An He 111Z-1 'twin' at Zaporozhe-South airfield during the supply operations for the cut-off Caucasus Front in January 1943. Note the large ▼ supplementary fuel containers

Right: The He 111Z-1s carried out their supply and evacuation tasks on the Eastern Front regardless of weather conditions ▶

Above: An He 111Z in readiness at Zaporozhe-South in winter 1942/43. *Below:* Paratroops waiting for their transport gliders for the transfer to the south of France in 1943.

that had been tested with the He 111 were used operationally for the first time, but without much success, by 12 Do 217E-5s of II/KG 100 against a British anti-submarine force in the Bay of Biscay. The subsequent use of these flying bombs was also unsuccessful. The main carrier aircraft for the Hs 293 were the Do 217 E-5 and He 177A-5.

On 9 September began the Allied Operation 'Avalanche', the landing of the US 5th Army under Lt General Clark at Salerno in southern Italy. At the same time the cease-fire between the Allies and the Italians came into force, whereupon German units in Italy disarmed the Italian troops and moved them to prisoner-of-war camps.

On the Eastern front, meanwhile, the continuous losses suffered had so weakened the German army formations that the Soviet forces managed to break through in a number of different places. The bomber units equipped with He 111 were continually having to supply cut-off troops with arms, ammunition and food. Where it was still possible to land, but the available space too restricted to permit the use of different places. The bomber units equipped with He 111s were continually having to supply cut-off troops with arms, ammunition and food. Where it was still possible to land, but the available space too restricted to permit the use of cargo gliders, the so-called 'DOBBAS' were used. These consisted of an aerodynamically-

For this purpose a carrier frame was attached to the ventral external bomb racks of either the He 111H-16 or the Ju 88A-4 from which the 'DOBBAS' was then slung. Where the landing strip was reasonably firm there was still enough ground clearance to allow the aircraft to land, but 'DOBBAS' could not be used where ground conditions were soft.

Between 12 and 15 November 1943 the German armed forces carried out their last successful combined operation involving all three arms of the services in the Mediterranean area. This was Operation *Leopard*, the landing of 'Combat Group Müller' commanded by a *Generalleutnant* of that name on the island of Leros in the Aegean. X *Fliegerkorps* under *General der Flieger* Geisler was able to muster 206 aircraft for this operation, including a few He 111s. Although successful, the German assault force lost 1,109 killed, wounded and missing amounting to 41% of the forces employed.

On 20 November the 3rd Ukrainian Front under Army General Malinovsky launched an offensive in the lower Dnieper area. Thanks to the support of every available bomber and Stuka *Geschwader* in this sector the defensive power of the German army units was so strengthened that they were able to prevent the Soviet forces breaking through. On 22 November the island of Samos in the Aegean was recaptured, thus bringing all the Dodecanese islands back into German hands. On the Eastern front too, the line was, on the whole, being held. But for how long? The German forces were weakened and overstretched and the superiority of the Allies was increasing all the time.

Brief mention has already been made regarding the use of the He 111 as provisional night fighters on the Eastern front. It was only a make-shift arrangement, but how successful they could be in this role was shown by an engagement fought by *Unteroffizier* Döring of 9. *Staffel*/KG 55 in the Stalingrad area: during a running fight he shot down three four-engined Tupolev TB-3 (ANT-6) night bombers with his He 111H-6.

At the end of 1943 a new version of the He 111 (which will be described later) was being flown by NJGr.10, NJG 101 and the so-called *Behelfs-Beleuchter-Staffeln* (Auxiliary illuminator flights). These aircraft, equipped with the FuG 220 SN-2 *Lichtenstein* AI radar and FuG 350 *Naxos* detection/homing devices were used as contact aircraft and 'target illuminators' in night fighter operations against the RAF bombers. As far as is known these machines were flown unarmed.

On 4 January 1944 the first Soviet troops crossed the Polish-Soviet border in a westerly direction at Sarny in Wolhinia. Ten days later began the great Soviet offensive against the northern sector of the Eastern Front, eventually leading to a break-through.

In the south the Allies had already reached central Italy. In this situation the night raid on London on 21/22 January by IX *Fliegerkorps* led by *Oberst* Peltz with 447 aircraft, among them some He 111 units, repeated the following night with 285 aircraft can only be seen as an expression of Hitler's impotent rage, for it was certainly without any military value. The fact that in February 1944 1,217 German fighters were lost illustrates how catastrophic the situation of the German Luftwaffe was when faced with the qualitative and quantitative Allied superiority. In mid-February the attempt to wipe out the Allied bridgehead at Anzio and Nettuno in southern Italy failed. Between 20 and 25 February came the 'Big Week', a series of bombing raids by the US Army Air Force directed primarily at the German aircraft and aero-engine industry. As in 1942, the Heinkel factory in Rostock-Marienehe was again badly hit.

In spite of this, the development of the He 111 proceeded and early in 1944 KG 40, stationed in the west, received the first He 111H-18. This version was a development of the He 111H-16/R3 with more improved radio

equipment. Its armament consisted of one 20 mm MG/FF cannon and up to five 7·9 mm MG 81 machine-guns. On account of the complicated electronic and navigational equipment the He 111H-18 was manned by a crew of six and the bomb-load was limited to only 1,000 kg. This version was also powered by Jumo 211F-2 engines.

The British made their first acquaintance with the He 111Z early in 1944 as is shown by the following report reaching Germany on 14 March 1944 via *Interavia*, the Swiss aeronautical press agency:

'British intruder aircraft returning from sorties over France reported shooting down a strange heavy towing aircraft of the German Luftwaffe being used as a tug for two Gotha Go 242 cargo gliders. This aircraft — whose existence has been rumoured for some time — consisted of two twin-engined He 111 bombers, each having had one wing removed, joined by a rectangular wing mid-section carrying three engines; the five-engined aircraft thus produced had crew accommodation in both fuselage sections, the two tail units not being interconnected. The reasons for this development apparently stems from the fact that the standard He 111 has insufficient power to tow two such gliders. Presumably the Heinkel model described is one of the experimental constructions undertaken by various different aircraft manufacturers dictated by the development of the first large transport gliders.'

On 27 March this report was supplemented by the following short announcement:

'According to a British report the designation of the specially designed five-engined Heinkel towing aircraft (cf *Interavia* No. 910) is Heinkel He 111Z'

As early as 1941 Siegfried Günter had been

working on a project designed substantially to improve the performance of the He 111 in all respects without radically changing the airframe itself. This could only be achieved by raising the output of the power plants. There was a choice of two new engines, the Daimler-Benz DB 603 and the Jumo 213, both expected to develop 1,750 hp. The problem lay in the fact that both these engines required larger radiators. The tunnel-type radiators with which the He 111 had, until then, been fitted were inadequate, or would have had to have been enlarged to such an extent that their drag would have gone a long way towards cancelling out the increased performance of the engines. Then it was decided to use annular radiators like those normally fitted on the Ju 88. Since the two new engines were not yet available use had to be made of the DB 601U units with TK 9AC superchargers.

The trials appear to have been carried out by Weser Flugzeugbau at their Lemwerder works since the construction specification for the experimental machine originated with this firm. This aircraft, the He 111V32, *Werk Nr.* 2122, registration D-APZD, was completed on 31 December 1941. The following details are taken from a Weserflug document:

'*General:* The above-mentioned airframe was fitted with two DB 601U engines with exhaust-driven superchargers. It was found necessary for this purpose to re-position the engine nacelles forward of the fire-wall and also to strengthen the engine mounting points. Calibrating equipment was installed in the cabin and the monitoring and operating instruments in the cockpit modified accordingly.

Power plants: Two DB 601U liquid-cooled 12-cylinder four-stroke fuel injection engines with DVL TK 9AC exhaust-driven turbo-superchargers.

Propellers: VDM three-bladed variable pitch with special Schwarz blades of 3·5 m (11 ft 5¾ in) diameter.

Cowling: The water and oil coolers for the engines are in the form of annular radiators and are situated immediately behind of the propellers.

This arrangement gives the engine fairing an almost cylindrical shape. A series of removable light-metal panels permits easy access to both the engines and to the turbo-supercharger.

Operating controls: The operating controls were largely those of the existing models adapted to meet the new requirements. The engine is regulated by a single-lever whereby the move of the hand lever first operates the throttle butterfly and then the exhaust control vent. Supercharger boost pressure limit is achieved by means of an altitude-compensated shut-off regulator coupled to the throttle linkage. This shut-off regulator is coupled to the throttle and exhaust regulator linkage in such a way that, in an emergency, it may be overriden by shearing a pin.

Exhaust system: The exhaust gases are collected in an exhaust manifold, fed into the turbine and thence via a bifurcated tube back into the atmosphere. Flexible expansion mountings are provided to take up heat expansion and engine vibration. Exhaust ducts situated inside the engine cowling are enveloped and insulated in quartz wool. The area of the exhaust shaft is cooled by air from the annular engine radiator. The right and left exhaust pipes are connected by a tie-line.'

But the tests did not go as expected. In fact, the whole history of German turbo-superchargers developed by Hirth-Motorenwerke, a subsidiary of the Heinkel concern, is one long tragedy. This develop-

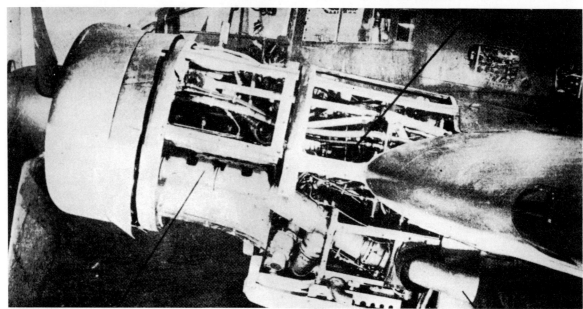

Left: The annular radiators fitted to the He 111V32 with the
DB 601U turbo-supercharged engines gave the aircraft a
completely new look

Above: An He 111H-16 waiting for the next operational
sortie on a roughly cleared airstrip in the East. Note the SC
50 bombs with 'Jericho trumpet' pipes in the foreground.
Below: An He 111H-16/U1 on operational flight. By that
time most Luftwaffe bombers either carried no unit code
letters and insignia at all, or displayed the code in very
small letters

ment, theoretically so efficient, failed time and again due to the shortage of suitable raw materials. Materials manufactured in Germany were simply incapable of withstanding the enormous temperatures developed by the engine exhaust gases driving the superchargers. Reading the reports on these tests it becomes obvious why no exhaust-driven turbo-superchargers able to function long enough to be of operational use were ever successfully developed in Germany. This chronic shortage of suitable alloys also explains why testing the He 111V32 had repeatedly to be suspended, finally resulting in the abandonment of the planned He 111R-1 and R-2 high-altitude bomber versions in 1944. An added reason for this was that the Emergency Fighter Programme also came into force in 1944 and all development work on bombers was stopped at the same time. All that remainded was the basic He 111, a reliable but by then rather aged airframe, a design overtaken by technical developments.

As a final attempt to breathe new life into it, the Heinkel works adapted it for the new Jumo 213 engines as the He 111H-21. A small series of these bombers were built powered by the Jumo 213E-1 engines developing 1,750 hp for take-off. With these power plants this final He 111 bomber version was capable of quite amazing performance, taking off with a bomb load of up to 3,000 kg (6,614 lb) without rocket assistance. Carrying a normal bomb load of 2,000 kg (4,410 lb) the He 111H-21 achieved a maximum speed of 480 km/h (298 mph). This achievement of the Heinkel engineers becomes all the more remarkable when one considers that the appreciably 'younger' Ju 188E-1 was only about 20 km/h (12·4 mph) faster. The He 111H-21 carried an armament of three 13 mm MG 131 and two MG 81Z machine-guns and went into full operational service as a night bomber in 1944.

The He 111H-20 that preceded it was a very versatile version delivered in four different variants:

He 111H-20/R1 transport for 16 paratroops with the same armament as the H-16 but without bomb racks;

He 111H-20/R2 night bomber, similar to the H-16 but equipped for glider-towing;

He 111H-20/R3 night bomber; more heavily armoured and with improved electronic equipment; and

He 111H-20/R4 night nuisance raider, similar to the H-20/R3 but with GM 1 injection for increased short duration power boost.

These aircraft were still in operational use in 1945.

The two initial variants, the He 111 H-20/R1 and /R2 proved their worth for the first time in evacuating the wounded from the pocket at Korsun, south-east of Cherkassy. As at Stalingrad, the He 111s were used as transports to supplement the Ju 52 which could not cope with the demand. Over 2,400 wounded were flown out, and in May 1944 when Sevastopol was evacuated He 111H-20s shared the task of transporting elements of the 17th Army from the Crimea to Romania. The Luftwaffe alone transported 21,457 troops, mainly wounded. On 25 May 1944, during the Operation *Rösselsprung* (Knight's Move), the unsuccessful attempt to capture the Yugoslav Communist partisan leader Tito and his staff, a number of He 111H-20/R2s were used to bring in the paratroops.

The invasion of Normandy began on 6 June and here too the German paratroops were brought in by He 111s.

On the night of 21/22 June a number of He 111s took part in a successful operation

By day and by night, with and without fighter cover and in spite of overwhelming numerical superiority of the Soviet Air Force, the He 111H-16/U1 bombers continued to fly their operations in support of the army

The *Dobbas* was an emergency solution to the problem of air supply of arms and other equipment. It was a shaped plywood container capable of carrying equipment up the size (and weight) of the 7·5 cm Pak 41 anti-tank gun, seen here, but was not used operationally to a great extent

against Allied bomber units. A formation of 114 Boeing B-17 Flying Fortresses escorted by 70 North American P-51 Mustangs of US 8th Army Air Force flew on eastwards after a major raid on Berlin, and 73 B-17s landed in Poltava, 41 in Mirgorod and the P-51s in Piryatin. However, the Americans were unaware that an He 177A-3 had attached itself to their formation and noted where the American aircraft had landed. IV *Fliegerkorps* under *Generalleutnant* Meister was alerted, and about 200 Ju 88 and He 111 bombers from KG 3, 4, 53 and 55 took off for the attack, with He 111H-16/R3s functioning as 'pathfinders'. Of this force, KG 4 and 55 were the only units flying the He 111H-16 and H-20/R2. This Luftwaffe raid was a great success: the Americans and Soviets were completely surprised, 47 B-17s were destroyed and most of the others so severely damaged as to be unfit for further service. The following night the Luftwaffe bombers came again and destroyed the complete American stockpile of bombs and fuel on Russian soil; only the P-51 Mustangs escaped this fate. After this disaster the Americans never again attempted another shuttle operation.

The He 111 was to demonstrate its efficiency in yet another field. The bombardment of London by the Fi 103 flying bombs had begun on 12 June 1944. During the development period these missiles were known as FZG 76 (*Flak Zielgerät* or anti aircraft gun target device 76), officially they became known as 'V1' (*Vergeltungswaffe* or Reprisal Weapon-1), but the actual RLM designation was Fi 103. Until 30 June Flak-Rgt. 155 which carried out this operation, had launched 2,000 of these missiles of which only 1,000 penetrated as far as the London area, most of these—661 to be exact—being shot down by British fighters or anti-aircraft guns. But the V 1 bombardment

continued. When it became obvious that the launching ramps in Holland were going to be overrun by the Allies, a make-shift carrier for this missile was evolved from the He 111H-21. The trusty He 111 proved amenable once again and was able to fulfil this unusual task as well. Designated He 111H-22, this modified version could carry and air-launch one Fi 103, but only a limited number of these machines were completed. There were also plans for launching manned V 1 missiles code-named *Reichenberg* from the He 111H-22, but these were never used operationally.

During the course of 1944 the He 111Z glider tugs were decimated: eight were shot down or destroyed on the ground by Allied fighter-bombers, leaving only four operational by the autumn. Two other versions of the 'twin He 111' had been projected by the RLM Technical Office before the stop was put to bomber production and development. The He 111Z-2 long-range bomber was intended to carry four SC 1800 or six SD 1000 bombs, or even four Hs 293 guided rocket-powered bombs, but was never built. The He 111Z-3 was a projected long-range reconnaissance version with an estimated range of 4,500 km (2,796 miles) but that, too, did not advance beyond the drawing board stage. In the event, the He 111H-23 was the last He 111 version actually built. Originally intended as paratroop transports, these machines were returned to the factory for reconversion to ordinary He 111H-20 bombers because there was no longer any likelihood of paratroop operations. Production of the He 111 finally ceased in the autumn of 1944.

The number of He 111s manufactured can only be estimated. A total of 12 He 111s were built for Lufthansa, and there were at least 32 experimental or V-series machines that were not delivered to the Luftwaffe. Production for

The surviving He 111H-8 'balloon cutters' of 1940/41 were modified afterwards and in service again in 1943/44 as glider towing aircraft. These pictured show He 111H-8/R-2s of *Schleppgruppe* 1 on the Eastern Front

Left: Soviet photograph of an He 111H-16 shot down near Narva in May 1944

Above: An He 111H-8/R2 of *Schleppgruppe* 4 at Pskov-South in winter 1943/44.
Below: He 111H-8/R2 with a DFS 230A glider in rigid tow

Above: He 111H-21 bombers were fitted with an electrically-operated dorsal turret mounting a 13 mm MG 131. *Below:* Three He 111H-20 bombers in winter 1943/44

He 111H-22 5K + GA of *Stab*/KG 3 with a Fieseler Fi 103 (V1) attached under the starboard wing root. Note the twin-barrel MG 81Z in beam position. In autumn 1944 such aircraft were used in the hazardous approach flights to the British Isles in an attempt to continue the Operation *Rumpelkammer*, launching some 110 missiles

the Luftwaffe amounted to 808 aircraft until September 1939, although according to Prof Heinkel's memoirs another 452 He 111s were built in 1939, giving a total of 1,260 aircraft. Known production figures for the subsequent years are as follows: 1940–756 aircraft; 1941–950; 1942–1,337; 1943–1,405; and 1944–756, making a grand total of 6,508 He 111s. According to the Luftwaffe Quartermaster-General's returns 5,656 He 111s were built during the war. Adding to this figure the 12 Lufthansa aircraft, 808 He 111s built before the war and the 32 V-series aircraft we reach the same total of 6,508 aircraft.

In conclusion, it is of interest to note what Prof Heinkel himself has written about the He 111:

'They became reliable, proven and easily-maintained worker-bees for the Luftwaffe bomber units. Even though, after 1941, they had been technically superseded and, above all, were hampered by their lack of range . . and, despite repeated modifications, could not be given the additional range required—there was really no substitute for them.'

Above: Trials with the *Reichenberg-Gerät* (manned Fi 103 or V1) carried out by an He 111H-18. *Below:* Fi 103 in position slung under the port wing of an He 111H-22

Left: He 111H-16 with an PC 1000 (2,205 lb) armour-piercing bomb. *Right:* A lineup of He 111H-10 bombers awaiting delivery

Below left: The Jumo 211F-2 engine with the broad-bladed Junkers variable-pitch propeller on an He 111H-16. *Right:* Jumo 211F-2 with the cowlings removed

Above: Aircrew of KG 55 getting ready for another operational flight. *Below:* He 111H-16s of KG 55 flying east

Two pictures that clearly show the external underfuselage PVC bomb racks on the later He 111H-series

Slovak paratroops boarding an H111H-20/R1 transport which could accommodate 16 paratroops and featured a ventral jump hatch

Left: A crash-landed He 111H-18 of *Sonderkommando Rastedter*, a special 'pathfinder' detachment of KG 40 in March 1944. The additional radio masts are clearly visible

Below: Newly completed He 111H-20s taxiing for take-off at Marienehe

Above: The RLM 65 light blue undersurfaces of this He 111H have been well blackened by engine exhaust gases. *Below:* Wreckage of an He 111H near Hirschberg in Silesia in May 1945

The victors: Two American airmen pose in front of an He 111H-20. Note the elongated muzzle flash hider of the nose MG-FF/M cannon

Centre: He 111H-5 D-ACLQ communications aircraft left behind after the capitulation of Axis forces in Tunisia in May 1943. *Bottom:* This He 111H-16 is now in the USA

Norwegian soldiers posing at an abandoned He 111H-18 in Norway in May 1945

Top: A crashed He 111H-3 found after the war in Gjönnervaansee that might be restored. *Centre and below:* These two He 111s have lain on Björnefell, near Narvik, since spring 1940

Epilogue

Alongside the historic aircraft on the Spectator's terrace at Frankfurt airport there is also an He 111. But, somehow, it seems strange to those who flew the He 111 on active service—almost, but not quite the same aircraft. In fact, it is not a German He 111 but one of the last machines built under licence in Spain by Construcciones Aeronauticas SA (CASA) in Seville. Altogether 236 were manufactured there designated CASA 2.111 HE. Initially, apart from their different camouflage, the Spanish He 111s were identical to the German He 111H-6 version as long as the Jumo 211 power plants could be delivered from Germany. After the end of the war this licence-built He 111 remained the standard bomber of the Spanish Air Force, and more aircraft were required. Production of the airframes presented no difficulties, but the engines were a problem. Eventually it was decided to fit the Rolls-Royce Merlin engines and the basic airframe was adapted accordingly. Of course, these new power plants also gave the Spanish He 111 a new look: the Jumo 211 had been a 12-cylinder inverted-V type engine, the Merlin was an upright-V type, and also required a larger radiator. The result was an He 111 with an airframe similar to the original design but looking rather strange because of its different engines.

The He 111 also continued to be flown in Eastern Europe after the end of the war. A number of He 111s left behind by the Luftwaffe in Romania were converted to passenger transports to meet the need for civil aircraft, and in Czechoslovakia some He 111H-6 bombers were impressed into Czech Air Force service, but they have all been scrapped long since. However, some 'real' He 111s are still in existence. If Britain were to open up her old arsenals at Farnborough an He 111 would certainly be found there. But until now all requests for one of the German aircraft packed away in crates there to be made available for exhibition in the German Museum at Munich have, alas, been made in vain.

◀ *Left top:* The oddly repainted Spanish-built He 111 with Rolls-Royce Merlin engines on the spectators' terrace at Frankfurt airport.
Centre: He 111H-5 destined for Romania. *Below:* An He 111H that found its way into the Czechoslovak Air Force after the war

▲ Two views of an HE 111H-5 in Romania that was converted to a passenger
▼ transport after the war

Above: The CASA 2.111 production line at Sevilla in Spain. The initial 130 aircraft had German Jumo 211F-2 engines *(below)*

Above: A Spanish-built CASA 2.111 B.I bomber (He 111H-6) with Jumo 211F-2 engines. *Centre:* CASA 2.111 B21 bomber with Rolls-Royce Merlin 500-29 engines, and *(below)* CASA 2.111 trainer/transport in Spanish Air Force service

Sources

Aders, Gebhard *Geschichte der deutschen Nachtjagd 1917–1945* Stuttgart, 1978 (English edition: *History of the German Night Fighter Force 1917–1945,* Jane's, 1979)
Aircraft of the Fighting Powers Vols. I and III Harborough
Bekker, Cajus *Angriffshöhe 4000* Hamburg, 1964 (English edition: *Luftwaffe War Diaries,* Macdonald & Jane's, 1967)
Ver Elst *De oorlog in de lucht en in de ruimte* Vols. II & III
Heinkel, Ernst *Stürmisches Leben* (English edition:
Graf Hoyos *Pedros y Pablos*
Nowarra, Heinz J. *Heinkel und seine Flugzeuge*
Nowarra-Kens *Die deutschen Flugzeuge 1933–45* München, 1972
Stroud *European Transport Aircraft*
P. St. John Turner *Heinkel*
Wundshammer *Flieger, Ritter, Helden*

Appendices

Data Tables

NA = Not available

Type	Bäumer B Via	He 64b	He 70C–1	He 70F–1	He 111A–0	He 111B–2	He 111C–01	He 111D–0
Purpose	Sports	Sports	Commercial	Rec. bomber	Med. bomber	Med. bomber	Commercial	Med. bomber
Crew	1	2	2 + 4	3	4	4	2 + 10	4
Engine	Wright L4	Argus As 8R	BMW VI 6,0Z	BMW VI 7,3Z	BMW VI 6,0Z	DB 600CG	BMW VI 6,0Z	DB 600Ga
Power	1 × 65 hp	1 × 150 hp	1 × 367 hp	1 × 750 hp	2 × 660 hp	2 × 880 hp	2 × 660 hp	2 × 1,050 hp
Span	9·00 m (26 ft 6¼ in)	9·80 m (32 ft 2 in)	14·80 m (48 ft 6½ in)	14·80 m (48 ft 6½ in)	22·60 m (74 ft 2 in)	22·60 m (74 ft 2 in)	22·60 m (74 ft 2 in)	22·60 m (74 ft 2 in)
Length	6·25 m (20 ft 6 in)	8·31 m (27 ft 3 in)	11·50 m (37 ft 8¾ in)	11·70 m (38 ft 5 in)	17·50 m (57 ft 5 in)	17·51 m (57 ft 5¼ in)	17·50 m (57 ft 5 in)	17·50 m (57 ft 5 in)
Height	—	2·06 m (6 ft 9 in)	3·10 m (10 ft 2¼ in)	3·10 m (10 ft 2¼ in)	4·10 m (13 ft 5½ in)	4·00 m (13 ft 1½ in)	4·10 m (13 ft 5½ in)	4·00 m (13 ft 1½ in)
Wing area	11·20 m² (120·6 ft²)	14·40 m² (155·0 ft²)	36·50 m² (392·88 ft²)	36·50 m² (392·88 ft²)	87·60 m² (942·92 ft²)	87·60 m² (942·92 ft²)	87·60 m² (942·92 ft²)	87·60 m² (942·92 ft²)
Weight empty	300 kg (661 lb)	458 kg (1,010 lb)	2,360 kg (5,203 lb)	2,300 kg (5,070 lb)	5,400 kg (11,905 lb)	5,840 kg (12,875 lb)	5,400 kg (11,905 lb)	6,000 kg (13,228 lb)
Weight loaded	570 kg (1,257 lb)	780 kg (1,720 lb)	3,370 kg (7,430 lb)	3,420 kg (7,540 lb)	8,220 kg (18,122 lb)	8,600 kg (18,960 lb)	9,610 kg (21,186 lb)	8,800 kg (19,400 lb)
Payload	270 kg (595 lb)	322 kg (710 lb)	1,010 kg (2,227 lb)	1120 kg (2,469 lb)	720 kg (1,587 lb)	2,760 kg (6,085 lb)	4,210 kg (9,281 lb)	2,800 kg (6,173 lb)
Max speed	230 kmh (143 mph)	245 kmh (152 mph)	362 kmh (225 mph)	355 kmh (221 mph)	310 kmh (193 mph)	370 kmh (230 mph)	310 kmh (193 mph)	410 kmh (255 mph)
Cruis. speed	180 kmh (112 mph)	222 kmh (138 mph)	326 kmh (203 mph)	335 kmh (208 mph)	270 kmh (168 mph)	310 kmh (193 mph)	270 kmh (168 mph)	340 kmh (211 mph)
Land. speed	80 kmh (50 mph)	52 kmh (23 mph)	110 kmh (68 mph)	105 kmh (65 mph)	110 kmh (68 mph)	115 kmh (71 mph)	110 kmh (68 mph)	115 kmh (71 mph)
Ceiling	6,400 m (21,000 ft)	6,000 m (19,690 ft)	5,700 m (18,700 ft)	5,250 m (17,220 ft)	4,800 m (15,750 ft)	6,700 m (21,980 ft)	4,800 m (15,750 ft)	5,000 m (18,370 ft)
Range	1,000 km (621 mls)	760 km 472 mls)	950 km (590 mls)	1,000 km (621 mls)	2,500 km (1,554 mls)	1,050 km (652 mls)	2,400 km (1,491 mls)	1,050 km (652 mls)
T/O distance	NA	130 m (427 ft)	NA	NA	NA	NA	510 m (1,670 ft)	NA
Land. distance	NA	120 m (394 ft)	NA	NA	NA	NA	600 m (1,968 ft)	NA
Equipment	—	—	—	FuG III	NA	FuG III	—	FuG III
Armament	—	—	—	1 × MG 15	3 × MG 15	3 × MG 15	—	3 × MG 15
Offensive load	—	—	—	—	500 kg (1,102 lb) bombs	1,500 kg (3,307 lb) bombs	—	1,200 kg (2,646 lb) bombs

Type	He 111E–1	He 111F–1	He 111G–0	He 111G–3	He 111G–5	He 111J–1	He 111P–2	He 111P–4
Purpose	Med. bomber	Med. bomber	Commercial	Commercial	Communications	Torp. bomber	Med. bomber	Med. bomber
Crew	4	4	2 + 10	2 + 10	2 + 10	4	4	5
Engine	Jumo 211A–1	Jumo 211A–3	BMW VI 6,0 ZU	BMW 132H	DB 601Aa	DB 601Aa	DB 601A	DB 601A
Power	2 × 1,000 hp	2 × 1,100 hp	2 × 660 hp	2 × 880 hp	2 × 1,150 hp	2 × 1,150 hp	2 × 1,150 hp	2 × 1,150 hp
Span	22·50 m (73 ft 9¾ in)	22·60 m (74 ft 2 in)	22·50 m (73 ft 9¾ in)	22·60 m (74 ft 2 in)	22·60 m (74 ft 2 in)	22·50 m (73 ft 9¾ in)	22·60 m (74 ft 2 in)	22·60 m (74 ft 2 in)
Length	17·50 m (57 ft 5 in)	17·50 m (57 ft 5 in)	17·30 m (56 ft 9 in)	17·20 m (56 ft 5¼ in)	17·10 m (56 ft 1 in)	16·40 m (53 ft 9½ in)	16·40 m (53 ft 9½ in)	16·40 m (53 ft 9½ in)
Height	4·20 m (13 ft 9¼ in)	4·20 m (13 ft 9¼ in)	4·20 m (13 ft 9¼ in)	4·10 m (13 ft 5½ in)	4·10 m (13 ft 5½ in)	4·20 m (13 ft 9¼ in)	4·00 m (13 ft 1½ in)	4·00 m (13 ft 1½ in)
Wing area	87·60 m² 942·92 ft²)	87·60 m² (942·92 ft²)	87·60 m² (942·92 ft²)	87·60 m² (942·92 ft²)	87·60 m² (942·92 ft²)	87·60 m² (942·92 ft²)	87·60 m² (942·92 ft²)	87·60 m² (942·92 ft²)
Weight empty	6,135 kg (13,525 lb)	6,200 kg (13,668 lb)	—	—	—	6,200 kg (13,668 lb)	6,020 kg (13,272 lb)	6,775 kg (14,936 lb)
Weight loaded	10,600 kg (23,369 lb)	10,600 kg (23,369 lb)	8,020 kg (17,681 lb)	8,460 kg (18,651 lb)	8,820 kg (19,445 lb)	10,600 kg (23,369 lb)	12,570 kg (27,712 lb)	13,500 kg (29,762 lb)
Payload	3,865 kg (8,521 lb)	3,800 kg (8,377 lb)	—	—	—	4,400 kg (9,700 lb)	6,550 kg (14,440 lb)	6,725 kg (14,826 lb)
Max speed	430 kmh (267 mph)	440 kmh (273 mph)	315 kmh (196 mph)	345 kmh (214 mph)	415 kmh (258 mph)	440 kmh (273 mph)	390 kmh (242 mph)	390 kmh (242 mph)
Cruis. speed	380 kmh (236 mph)	385 kmh (239 mph)	270 kmh (168 mph)	300 kmh (186 mph)	275 kmh (171 mph)	360 kmh (224 mph)	310 kmh (193 mph)	313 kmh (194 mph)
Land. speed	120 kmh (75 mph)	120 kmh (75 mph)	115 kmh (71 mph)	120 kmh (75 mph)	125 kmh (78 mph)	120 kmh (75 mph)	120 kmh (75 mph)	115 kmh (71 mph)
Ceiling	5,800 m (19,030 ft)	6,000 m (19,690 ft)	4,200 m (13,780 ft)	8,390 m (27,530 ft)	6,000 m (19,690 ft)	5,200 m (17,060 ft)	4,300/7,800 m (14,110/25,590 ft)	4,500/8,000 m (14,760/26,250 ft)
Range	1,820 km (1,131 mls)	1,820 km (1,131 mls)	1,000 km (621 mls)	1,500 km (932 mls)	1,500 km (932 mls)	1,800 km (1,118 mls)	2,100 km (1,305 mls)	2,090 km (1,299 mls)
T/O distance	NA	NA	NA	NA	NA	NA	1,300 m (4,265 ft)	1,300 m (4,265 ft)
Land. distance	NA	NA	NA	NA	NA	NA	1,050 m (3,445 ft)	1,000 m (3,280 ft)
Equipment	FuG III	FuG III	—	—	—	FuG III	FuG 10	FuG 10
Armament	3 × MG 15	3 × MG 15	—	—	—	3 × MG 15	4-5 × MG 15	6 × MG 15 1 × MG 17
Offensive load	2,000 kg (4,410 lb) bombs	2,000 kg (4,410 lb) bombs	—	—	—	1 × LT F5 torpedo	1,500 kg (3,307 lb) bombs	1,500 kg (3,307 lb) bombs

250

Type	He 111H–1	He 111H–3	He 111H–6	He 111H–16	He 111H–18	He 111H–20	He 111H–22	He 111Z–1	CASA C–2.111B (B.2l)
Purpose	Med. bomber	Med. bomber	Torp. bomber	Med. bomber	Night bomber	Transport	Med. bomber	Glider tug	Med. bomber
Crew	4	5	5	5	6	3 + 16	5	7	5
Engines	Jumo 211A–1	Jumo 211D–1	Jumo 211F–1	Jumo 211F–2	Jumo 211F–2	Jumo 211F–2	Jumo 213E–1	Jumo 211F–2	Rolls-Royce Merlin 500–29
Power	2 × 1,000 hp	2 × 1,200 hp	2 × 1,300 hp	2 × 1,340 hp	2 × 1,340 hp	2 × 1,340 hp	2 × 1,750 hp	5 × 1,340 hp	2 × 1,600 hp
Span	22·60 m (74 ft 2 in)	22·60 m (74 ft 2 in)	22·60 m (74 ft 2 in)	22·60 m (74 ft 2 in)	22·60 m (74 ft 2 in)	22·60 m (74 ft 2 in)	22·60 m (74 ft 2 in)	35·40 m (116 ft 2 in)	22·60 m (74 ft 2 in)
Length	16·40 m (53 ft 9½ in)	16·40 m (53 ft 9½ in)	16·40 m (53 ft 9½ in)	16·40 m (53 ft 9½ in)	16·40 m (53 ft 9½ in)	16·40 m (53 ft 9½ in)	16·40 m (53 ft 9½ in)	16·69 m (54 ft 9 in)	16·40 m (53 ft 9½ in)
Height	4·00 m (13 ft 1½ in)	4·00 m (13 ft 1½ in)	4·00 m (13 ft 1½ in)	4·00 m (13 ft 1½ in)	4·00 m (13 ft 1½ in)	4·00 m (13 ft 1½ in)	4·00 m (13 ft 1½ in)	4·53 m (14 ft 10 in)	4·00 m (36 ft 1½ in)
Wing area	87·60 m² (842·92 ft²)	87·60 m² (942·92 ft²)	87·60 m² (942·92 ft²)	87·60 m² (942·92 ft²)	87·60 m² (942·92 ft²)	87·60 m² (942·92 ft²)	87·60 m² (942·92 ft²)	147·0 m² (1,582·3 ft²)	87·60 m² (942·92 ft²)
Weight empty	6,740 kg (14,859 lb)	7,200 kg (15,873 lb)	8,680 kg (19,136 lb)	8,680 kg (19,136 lb)	8,680 kg (19,136 lb)	8,680 kg (19,136 lb)	10,500 kg (23,148 lb)	21,400 kg (47,178 lb)	8,570 kg (18,893 lb)
Weight loaded	12,600 kg (27,778 lb)	13,120 kg (28,924 lb)	14,000 kg (30,864 lb)	14,000 kg (30,864 lb)	14,000 kg (30,864 lb)	14,000 kg (30,864 lb)	15,930 kg (35,119 lb)	28,400 kg max (62,611 lb)	14,000 kg (30,864 lb)
Payload	5,860 kg (12,919 lb)	5,920 kg (13,057 lb)	5,320 kg (11,728 lb)	5,320 kg (11,728 lb)	5,320 kg (11,728 lb)	5,320 kg (11,728 lb)	5,430 kg (11,971 lb)	7,000 kg max (15,432 lb)	5,430 kg (11,971 lb)
Max speed	410 kmh (255 mph)	440 kmh (273 mph)	440 kmh (273 mph)	435 kmh (270 mph)	435 kmh (270 mph)	440 kmh (273 mph)	475 kmh (295 mph)	435 kmh (270 mph)	408 kmh (253 mph)
Cruis. speed	325 kmh (202 mph)	330 kmh (205 mph)	330 kmh (205 mph)	330 kmh (205 mph)	330 kmh (205 mph)	330 kmh (205 mph)	370 kmh (230 mph)	392 kmh (244 mph)	315 kmh (136 mph)
Land. speed	125 kmh (78 mph)	125 kmh (78 mph)	125 kmh (78 mph)	130 kmh (81 mph)	130 kmh (81 mph)	130 kmh (81 mph)	135 kmh (84 mph)	130 kmh (81 mph)	125 kmh (77·6 mph)
Ceiling	6,500 m (21,330 ft)	8,000 m (26,250 ft)	6,500 m (21,330 ft)	6,700 m (21,980 ft)	6,700 m (21,980 ft)	6,500 m (21,330 ft)	10,000 m (32,810 ft)	10,000 m (32,810 ft)	6,700 m (21,980 ft)
Range	2,000 km (1,243 mls)	2,300 km (1,429 mls)	2,300 km (1,429 mls)	2,900 km (1,802 mls)	2,300 km (1,429 mls)	2,250 km (1,398 mls)	2,900 km (1,802 mls)	2,000 km (1,243 mls)	2,255 km (1,401 mls)
T/O distance	1,000 m (3,280 ft)	1,100 m (3,610 ft)	1,100 m (3,610 ft)	1,150 m (3,770 ft)	1,150 m (3,770 ft)	1,200 m (3,940 ft)	1,100 m (3,610 ft)	1,500 m (4,920 ft)	1,895 m (6,217 ft)
Land. distance	NA	NA	NA	NA	NA	NA	NA	NA	1,180 m (3,870 ft)
Equipment	FuG III	FuG 10	FuG 10	FuG 10, FuG 16	FuG 10, FuG 16, FuG 101, FuG 227	FuG 10, FuG 16	FuG 10, FuG 16	FuG 10, FuG 16	HF, VHF, UHF, ADF + radio compass
Armament	3 × MG 15	1 × MG–FF 6 × MG 15	1 × MG–FF 5 × MG 15 1 × MG 17	1 × MG–FF 1 × MG 131 3 × MG 81Z	1 × MG–FF 4-5 × MG 81	1 × MG–FF 1 × MG 131 3 × MG 81Z	3 × MG 131 1 × MG 81Z	2 × MG 131 4 × MG 81 2 × MG 81Z	NA
Offensive load	2,000 kg (4,410 lb) bombs	2,000 kg (4,410 lb) bombs	2,000 kg (4,410 lb) bombs or 2 × LT F5 torpedoes	3,000 kg (6,614 lb) bombs max	NA	—	3,000 kg (6,614 lb) bombs max or 1 × Fi 103	—	2,000 kg (4,410 lb) bombs

251

Luftwaffe units wholly or partly equipped with the He 111 1939-1945

(compiled by the Editor)

Unit/formation	Code	Remarks
Aufkl.Gr.120	A6 +	⎫
Aufkl.Gr.121	7A +	⎬ Used He 111 together with Do 17 and Ju 88A until 1942
Aufkl.Gr.123	4U +	⎭
Aufkl.Gr.Ob.d.L.	T5 +	'Gruppe Rowehl'; last He 111 replaced in 1942
KG 1 *Hindenburg*	V4 +	*Stab*/I/II Gruppen only until late 1940
KG 3 *'Blitz'*	5K +	III/KG 3 first to launch Fi 103 in July 1944
KG 4 *General Wever*	5J +	Retained He 111 in transport role until April 1945
KG 26 *'Löwengeschwader'*	1H +	Only Luftwaffe torpedo-bomber unit
KG 27 *Boelcke*	1G +	Used He 111 until disbanded in July 1944
KG 28	1T +	II/KG 28 only; 'Pathfinder' unit
KG 40	F8 +	III/KG 40 until late 1941; I/KG 40 in part until 1943
KG 51 *Edelweiss*	9K +	Converted to Ju 88A in summer 1940
KG 53 *Legion Condor*	A1 +	Changed to Fi 103 launching operations in September
KG 54 *Totenkopf*	B3 +	Converted to Ju 88A by late 1940
KG 55 *Greif*	G1 +	Withdrawn from operations July 1944 for retraining on Bf 109 and FW 190 as KG(J) 55
KG 76	F1 +	I/KG 76 with He 111H-10 late in 1941
KG 100 *Wiking*	6N +	I/KG 100 with He 111 until March 1943
KG 101	5T +	ex-KSG 1; semi-operational training unit
KGr.100	6N +	'Pathfinder' *Gruppe*; became part of KG 100
KGr.126	1T +	Became KGr.128
KGr.806	M7 +	ex-Kü.Fl.Gr.806
KSG 1 (later KG 101)	5T +	In part only
KSG 2	A8 +	Torpedo-bomber school Grosetto/Italy in 1942
Kü.Fl.Gr.806	M7 +	Spring 1941 became KGr.806
KGr.zbV 5	L5 +	Also code S3 +; May 1943 became TGr.30
KGr.zbV 20	?	Temporary formation during Stalingrad crisis
KGr.zbV 23	F3 +	As above
KGr.zbV 25	?	As above
LG 1	L1 +	III/LG 1 retained He 111 until August 1940
LG 2	L2 +	10.(K)/LG 2 with He 111 until October 1939
NJG 101	9W +	As trainers for AI radar operators
NNJ *Schwarm Ost*	8V +	Close-range night fighters on the Eastern Front 1942-43
TGr.30	S3 +	ex-KGr zbV 5; still operational in April 1945
TGr.111	?	Operational 1944
Wekusta 5	1A +	Weather reconnaissance until Vaernes/Norway
Wekusta 26	5M +	Also code 5Z +; in part only
Gruppe Uhl	?	Only unit still using He 111 offensively (against railway targets at night) in April 1945

In addition to that He 111s of different versions were flown in company with other types by *Fliegerverbindungsgeschwader* 1 and 2 (communications and liaison formations), most *Schleppgruppen* (glider tug units), *Flugbereitschaften* (stand-by flying units), several *Kurierstaffeln* (courier flights), *Luftnachrichten-Komp.* (Luftwaffe signals companies), *Versuchsverband Ob.d.L.,* various *Fliegerkorps* staff flights, test establishments, all blind-flying schools and other training formations.

Glossary

Luftwaffe units

As there are no accurate equivalents, this translation has kept the original Luftwaffe unit designations which are explained below.

The basic operational unit in the Luftwaffe was the *Gruppe*. Depending on the aircraft type (fighters, bombers, reconnaissance, coastal aviation) a *Gruppe* could comprise three to four *Staffeln* of nine to 16 aircraft each. Including its *Stab* (Staff Flight) of three to four machines a *Gruppe* had an establishment strength of 30 to 68 aircraft. However, the actual strength was often below the establishment, particularly during the last year of the war.

Certain *Gruppen* were formed as, and remained, independent formations. Their basic function was indicated by an abbreviation, thus: *Aufklärungsgruppe* (Aufkl.Gr.) = reconnaissance; *Jagd-* (JGr.) = fighters; *Kampf-* (KGr.) = bombers; *Küstenflieger-* (Kü.Fl.Gr.) = coastal aviation; *Nachtjagd-* (NJGr.) = night fighters; and *Schlepp- (S-Gruppe)* = glider tugs. KGr.z.b.V. *(Kampfgruppe zur besonderen Verwendung* or KGr. 'for special duties'*)* indicated a transport *Gruppe* of varying strength.

A *Geschwader* had a nominal strength of three to four *Gruppen* plus a *Stab*. As in the case of *Gruppen*, the establishment strength depended on the type of aircraft and the basic role, and could vary from 120 to over 200 aircraft. The actual strength was usually lower, being affected by such factors as combat losses, delayed replacements and (quite often) lack of matériel and aircrews in the first place. As with *Gruppen*, the basic function was indicated by an abbreviated prefix, thus: JG *(Jagdgeschwader)* = fighters; KG *(Kampf-)* = bombers; NJG *(Nachtjagd-)* = night fighters; SG *(Schlacht-)* = close support (before October 1943: St.G = *Stukageschwader*); and TG *(Transportgeschwader)* (after October 1943).

The *Gruppen* within a *Geschwader* were indicated by Roman numerals before the unit designation and the *Staffeln* — by Arabic numerals. Thus I/KG 4 = I *Gruppe* of KG 4; 9./KG 55 = 9.*Staffel* of KG 55 (part of III/KG 55).

Equivalent ranks

Luftwaffe	RAF	USAAF
Generalfeldmarschall	Marshal of the RAF	General (five star)
Generaloberst	Air Chief Marshal	General (four star)
General der Flieger	Air Marshal	Lieutenant General
Generalleutnant	Air Vice Marshal	Major General
Oberst	Group Captain	Colonel
Oberstleutnant	Wing Commander	Lieutenant Colonel
Major	Squadron Leader	Major
Hauptmann	Flight Lieutenant	Captain
Oberleutnant	Flying Officer	First Lieutenant
Leutnant	Pilot Officer	Second Lieutenant
Oberfähnrich	Officer Cadet	Officer Cadet
Oberfeldwebel	Flight Sergeant	Master Sergeant
Unteroffizier	Corporal	Corporal
Gefreiter	LAC	Private 1st Class

General Index

Heinkel He 111

Aircraft types